Ser   00099   /14
5 November 1968

~~TOP SECRET~~ - RESTRICTED DATA

SEVENTH ENDORSEMENT on Vice Admiral   , U. S.
Navy (Retired) 058722/1103 (TS-RESDATA) ltr of 25 July 1968

From: Commander in Chief U. S. Atlantic Fleet
To: Vice Admiral   U. S. Navy (Retired)
      058722/1103

Subj: Court of Inquiry to inquire into the circumstances sur-
      rounding the loss of USS SCORPION (SSN 589) on or about
      27 May 1968 (U)

1. (U) The Report of Proceedings of the Court of Inquiry less
Annex A is returned for further investigation and evaluation of
newly discovered evidence in connection with subject loss.

2. (U) Upon completion of the additional proceedings, it is
requested that the entire record of proceedings and a supplemental
report be submitted to this command.

Copy to:
CNO
CINCPACFLT
COMSUBPAC
COMSUBLANT
JAG
SUBSAFECEN

Group 3
Downgrading at 12 year intervals
Not automatically declassified
DOD DIR 5200.10

JAG- CNA-17-69

DEPARTMENT OF THE NAVY
OFFICE OF THE JUDGE ADVOCATE GENERAL
WASHINGTON, D. C. 20370

IN REPLY REFER TO
JAG: 21: HAW: ah
Ser#00011-68
4 November 1968

~~TOP SECRET~~

TOP SEC___ (UNCLASSIFIED UPON REMOVAL OF BASIC CORRESPONDENCE)

SIXTH ENDORSEMENT on subject record

From: Judge Advocate General
To: Commander in Chief U. S. Atlantic Fleet

Subj: Court of Inquiry into loss of USS SCORPION (U)

1. (U) Forwarded for use in connection with the reconvened Court of Inquiry.

B4

I
Acting Judge Advocate General

~~TOP SECRET~~

JAG-CNA-17-69

Op-311G/cw
Ser 00036P31
5 NOV 1968

~~SECRET~~ (Declassified upon removal of basic correspondende
and endorsements)

FIFTH ENDORSEMENT on Vice Admiral   B4 ___   USN(RET.),
058722/1103, 1tr of 25 Jul 1968

From: Chief of Naval Operations
To: Judge Advocate General

Subj: Court of Inquiry into loss of USS SCORPION (U)

1.   (U) The original record is forwarded without Annex "A".
It is felt that the material contained in annex "A" is not
pertinent to the further proceedings under the Convening
Authority's order reconvening the Court of Inquiry and will
be retained in OPNAV for security reasons.

B4

Deputy Chief of Naval Operations
(Fleet Operations and Readiness)

Copy to:
OP-00
OP-09

Copy _/_ of _8_ copies
Page _/_ of _/_ pages

JAG-CNA-17-69

DECLASSIFIED

~~TOP SECRET -- RESTRICTED DATA~~
(Unclassified upon removal
of basic correspondence)

2 5 SEP 1969

FOURTH ENDORSEMENT on Vice Admiral   , U. S. Navy
(Retired), ltr of 19 Dec 1968 (Top Secret -- Restricted Data)

From: Secretary of the Navy
To: Judge Advocate General

Subj: Court of Inquiry to inquire into the circumstances surround-
      ing the loss of USS SCORPION (SSN-589) on or about 27 May 1968

Encl: (4) Copy of SECNAV ltr of 25 Sep 1969 to Chairman, Joint
          Committee on Atomic Energy

1. The basic correspondence and prior endorsements have served the
purposes for which they were submitted directly to the Secretary of
the Navy. They are forwarded for such further disposition as may be
appropriate.

2. By letter of this date to the Chairman of the Joint Committee on
Atomic Energy, copy appended as enclosure (4), I have agreed to make
available to that Committee the complete supplemented record of
proceedings of the subject Court of Inquiry, including the Court's
findings of fact, opinions, and recommendations and the actions of
the convening authority. It is requested that the Judge Advocate
General contact Mr.   , Director of the Committee staff,
and make the necessary arrangements accordingly.

3. It is requested that a copy of the material provided to the Joint
Committee on Atomic Energy also be made available for the use of the
Atomic Energy Commission pursuant to the earlier request of the Commission
for access to the record of proceedings.

Copy to:
CNO

DECLASSIFIED

COPY No. _1_ of _2_ Copies ~~TOP SECRET~~

SecNav Conf. No. TS-123

~~TOP SECRET -- RESTRICTED DATA~~
(Unclassified upon removal
of basic correspondence)

JAG - CNA - 17-69

DECLASSIFIED (SECRET upon removal of
basic correspondence)

THIRD ENDORSEMENT on Vice Admiral   B C   U.S. Navy
(Retired), 058722/1103 (TS-Res Data) ltr of 19 Dec 1968

From: Chief of Naval Operations
To: Secretary of the Navy

Subj: Court of Inquiry into loss of USS SCORPION (U)

Encl: (1) Proposed SECNAV ltr to Chairman, Joint Committee
            on Atomic Energy

1.   (U) Forwarded for information and return to the Judge
Advocate General.

2.   (U) The Record of Proceedings of the USS SCORPION Court
of Inquiry has been reviewed within the Navy Department.
With data available to date, the exact cause of the loss
of SCORPION has not been determined.

3.   (U) Annex A and Supplementary Annex A have been removed
from the Record of the Court of Inquiry and are being retained
in OPNAV in the spaces set aside for stowage of information of
special sensitivity. I will make arrangements for these annexes
to be provided for your review at your convenience. However,
it should be noted that these annexes do not add to the understanding of the facts concerning the loss of SCORPION.

4.   (U) Action is in progress to further examine the SCORPION
wreckage, utilizing the deep diving submersible TRIESTE II.
It is hoped that close examination of the hull sections and
other debris by TRIESTE may provide additional information
useful in determining the nature and cause of the casualty.
The debris inspection, by TRIESTE II, is scheduled to commence in May 1969 and continue for a period of about four
months. I will inform you if any information of value in
determining the cause of SCORPION's loss evolves from TRIESTE
operations.

5.   (U) Recommendations made by the Court of Inquiry are
being considered for action, and I will advise you of those
actions later.

DECLASSIFIED

Page 1 of 2 Pages
Copy 1 of 5 Copies

~~TOP SECRET~~

TOP SECRET
JAG-CNA-17-69
Attachment (1) to
SecNav Cont. No. B-123

~~TOP SECRET~~

6.   (C) Enclosure (1) is a proposed letter to the Joint Committee on Atomic Energy which states that the record of the SCORPION Court of Inquiry will be made available without Annex A and Supplementary Annex A. Withholding of these annexes from the JCAE is recommended for the following reasons:

    a. It is not recommended that Annex A and Supplementary Annex A be given to the JCAE due to the sensitive nature of the material contained therein.

    b. These annexes do not add to the understanding of the facts concerning the loss of SCORPION.

    c. During informal discussions Mr. B6   , Executive Director, Joint Committee on Atomic Energy, agreed that the annexes should not be forwarded to the JCAE.

7.   (U) I recommend that you sign enclosure (1).

B6

6

DEPARTMENT OF THE NAVY
OFFICE OF THE JUDGE ADVOCATE GENERAL
WASHINGTON, D. C. 2....

IN REPLY REFER TO
JAG: 21: HAW: ah
Serial #000569

JAN 2 7 1969

~~TOP SE~~ - (UNCLASSIFIED UPON REMOVAL OF BASIC CORRESPONDENCE
AND PRECEDING AND SUCCEEDING ENDORSEMENTS)

SECOND ENDORSEMENT on Vice ___B4___ ., U. S. Navy
(Retired), 058722/1103 (TS-Res Data) ltr of 19 Dec 1968

From: Judge Advocate General
To: Secretary of the Navy
Via: Chief of Naval Operations

Subj: Court of Inquiry into loss of USS SCORPION (U)

1. (U) Forwarded for information, for such intermediate routing
or reference as the Chief of Naval Operations may deem indicated,
and for ultimate return to the Judge Advocate General. The
Chairman of the Joint Committee on Atomic Energy has requested
that the record of proceedings, findings, opinion, recommendations,
and action of the convening authority be made available to that
committee. The Judge Advocate General has recommended that the
Secretary advise the Chairman in essence, that a properly authorized
member of his staff consult with the Deputy Assistant Judge Advocate
General (Investigations) concerning details of access. If the
Chairman is so advised, the original record may be required on short
notice.

2. (U) Both in its original and reconvened sessions, subject Court
of Inquiry appears to have been convened, its proceedings conducted,
and its report rendered, in substantial compliance with Title 10,
U. S. Code, Section 935, regulations implementing that statute
contained in the Manual of the Judge Advocate General, and pertinent
provisions of other regulations, manuals, and instructions of the
Department of the Navy.

B4

Acting Judge Advocate General

Page 1 of 1 page

~~TOP SECRET~~

JAG-CNA-1719

19 December 1968

From: Vice Admiral   Blc   U.S. Navy (Retired) 058722/1103
To: Commander In Chief, U.S. Atlantic Fleet

Subj: Court of Inquiry to inquire into the circumstances surrounding
      the loss of USS SCORPION (SSN 589) on or about 27 May 1968

Ref: (a) CINCLANTFLT SEVENTH END ser 00099/14 of 5 Nov 1968 on record
          of subject Court

Encl: (1) Original record of proceedings, less Annex A, with seven
          endorsements thereto
      (2) Supplementary record of proceedings

1. As directed by reference (a) the Court of Inquiry was reconvened on
6 November 1968 to consider new evidence which had come to light since
the Court adjourned on 25 July 1968.

2. The original record of proceedings plus a supplementary record of
proceedings are forwarded herewith as enclosures (1) and (2). Annex A
to enclosure (2) contains matter considered to be of a sensitive nature,
access to which should be restricted to persons who need to know, and
is submitted in this form to permit removal as appropriate for future
routing.

3. The Court examined all new evidence in great detail and in addition
reviewed carefully its previous report. Where the new evidence required
modification of original findings of fact, opinions or recommendations
this has been reflected in the supplementary report.

4. The Court adjourned this date.

Blc

JAG-CNA-17-69

25 JUL 1968

From: Vice Admiral   : U.S. Navy (Retired)
        058722/1103
To: Commander in Chief, U.S. Atlantic Fleet

Subj: Court of Inquiry to inquire into the circumstances
        surrounding the loss of USS SCORPION (SSN589) on or
        about 27 May 1968

Ref: (a) CINCLANTFLT Appointing Order ltr ser 3123/142 of
            4 June 1968

Encl: (1) Subject Record of Proceedings
        (2) Unclassified Summary of Daily Proceedings
        (3) Classified Summary of Daily Proceedings

1. As directed by reference (a), a Court of Inquiry was convened
on 5 June 1968. The original record and nine complete copies
thereof are forwarded herewith as enclosure (1).

2. Annex A to enclosure (1) contains matter considered to be of
a sensitive nature, access to which should be restricted to persons
who need to know, and is submitted in this form to permit removal
as appropriate for future routing.

3. The court explored all possibilities which could be envisioned
in view of the obvious difficulties involved in determining the
exact cause of loss. In this pursuit, much was learned of the
practices and procedures followed in SCORPION in all areas. A
good overview of her material condition was presented and considered. Each area of probability was probed in depth.

4. Enclosures (2) and (3) provide a daily chronology of the
court's activities and, while not a part of the official record,
are submitted for such use as the convening authority may deem
appropriate.

5. The court has adjourned this date to await the pleasure of
the convening authority.

~~TOP SECRET~~

~~TOP SECRET~~ (Declassified upon removal of
basic correspondence and endorsements)

FOURTH ENDORSEMENT on Vice Admiral   ——— USN (RET.),
058722/1103, ltr of 25 Jul 1968

From: Secretary of the Navy
To: Judge Advocate General
Via: Chief of Naval Operations

Subj: Court of Inquiry into loss of USS SCORPION (U)

1. (U) The original record is returned for use in connection
with further proceedings under the Convening Authority's order
reconvening the Court of Inquiry. It is returned via the Chief of
Naval Operations to permit the reattachment of Annex "A", which was
not physically received in the Office of the Secretary of the Navy.

2. (U) It is requested that the revised or augmented record be
resubmitted to the Secretary of the Navy upon completion of further
proceedings and field and Departmental review.

Secretary of the Navy

~~TOP SECRET~~

~~TOP SECRET~~ (Declassified upon
removal of basic corres-
pondence and endorsements

Copy _/_ of _5_ copies

Page 1 of 1 page

003073

OP-00 CONTROL NO.

JAG-CNA-17-69

SecNav Cont No. *TS*

TOP SECRET (Downgraded to CONFIDENTIAL upon
removal of basic correspondence
and endorsements)

Ser 00034P31
18 OCT 1968

THIRD ENDORSEMENT on Vice Admiral   , USN(RET),
058722/1103 ltr of 25 Jul 1968

From: Chief of Naval Operations
To: Secretary of the Navy

Subj: Court of Inquiry into loss of USS SCORPION (U)

1. (U) The record of the USS SCORPION Court of Inquiry has
been reviewed by the Office of the Chief of Naval Operations,
Naval Ordnance Systems Command, Naval Ship Systems Command and
the Oceanographer of the Navy.

2. (U) The Chief of Naval Operations concurs with the Court's
opinion that the certain cause for the loss of SCORPION is not
ascertainable from any evidence now available. Based on the
evidence available, and the recommendation of CINCLANTFLT,
total commitment to any of the scenarios contained in the record
is not warranted.

3. (C) The Court's recommendations address themselves to corrective measures not only for practices, conditions, and deficiencies associated with the most probable causes of SCORPION's loss,
but also to those which were identified with the analysis of
less likely causes of her loss. Comments on the Court's opinions and recommendations from the Naval Ordnance Systems Command, Naval Ship Systems Command and the Oceanographer of the
Navy are being reviewed in OPNAV. Appropriate action on the
Court's recommendations will be taken after completion of this
review.

7

page 1 of 1 Pages
Copy 1 of 7 Copies

Attachment 3 to
SecNav Cont. No. 75-462

JAG-CNO-17-19

DEPARTMENT OF THE NAVY
OFFICE OF THE JUDGE ADVOCATE GENERAL
WASHINGTON, D. C. 20370

RESTRICTED DATA
Atomic Energy Act of 1954

UNCLASSIFIED

IN REPLY REFER TO
JAG:21:HAW:ah
Ser #0006-68
SEP 4 1968

~~TOP SECRET~~ (UNCLASSIFIED UPON REMOVAL OF BASIC CORRESPONDENCE)

SECOND ENDORSEMENT on subject record

From: Judge Advocate General
To: Secretary of the Navy
Via: Chief of Naval Operations

Subj: Court of Inquiry into loss of USS SCORPION (U)

1. (U) Forwarded for information and ultimate return.

2. (U) Subject Court of Inquiry appears to have been convened, its proceedings conducted, and its report rendered, in substantial compliance with Title 10, U. S. Code, section 935, regulations implementing that statute contained in the Manual of the Judge Advocate General, and pertinent provisions of other regulations, manuals and instructions of the Department of the Navy.

B6

UNCLASSIFIED

~~TOP SECRET~~

JAG-CNA-17-69.

Attachment (9) to
SecNav Cont. No. 75-

Page 1 of 1 page

~~TOP SECRET~~

Ser 00074 /14
15 August 1968

RESTRICTED DATA
ATOMIC ENERGY ACT = 1954

~~CONFIDENTIAL~~

~~TOP SECRET~~ - RESTRICTED DATA

FIRST ENDORSEMENT on Vice Admiral [B] , U. S. Navy
(Retired) 058722/1103 (TOP SECRET-RESTRICTED DATA) ltr of
25 July 1968

From: Commander in Chief U. S. Atlantic Fleet
To: Judge Advocate General

Subj: Court of Inquiry to inquire into the circumstances
      surrounding the loss of USS SCORPION (SSN 589) on or
      about 27 May 1968 (U)

1. (X) The Record of Proceedings of the Court of Inquiry which was
convened to inquire into the loss of the USS SCORPION (SSN 589) on
or about 27 May 1968 has been meticulously and thoroughly reviewed.
The Commander in Chief U. S. Atlantic Fleet is keenly aware of the
fact that there is a paucity of "hard" facts surrounding this
tragic incident, but considers that the Court of Inquiry and all
personnel connected therewith have competently and thoroughly
collected and recorded all reasonably relevant factual data and on
the basis of such data have well substantiated every reasonable
hypothesis of the manner in which this loss occurred.

2. (C) With respect to Recommendation 2 of the Report, the
Commander in Chief U. S. Atlantic Fleet concurs in principle that
NAVOCEANO's proposed system of Notices to Submerged Mariners be
implemented, however, caution should be exercised in accepting as
authentic "all source" information. Specifically, prior to the
issuance of new charts based on information received from spurious
sources, e.g., one-time soundings which are at variance with
published charts such as the 13-fathom sounding at Cruiser Banks
verification should be obtained.

3. (C) With respect to Recommendation 4 of the Report which con-
cerns the enhancement of "submerged navigational ability and to
provide increased safety from submerged groundings, all high speed
SSNs should be provided with [B/]   . it is
realized that [B/]

                Although [B/   ] may be presently
[   ] up to the maximum speed of the vessel, there is no approved
plan to develop or install any type of [B/]   1-
                ] in attack class submarines. The provision of [
[B/]   ] for all submerged speed ranges of a submarine
would greatly enhance the tactical navigational ability of combatant

Downgrade to ~~SECRET~~
By authority of OP-095/Op223   ~~CONFIDENTIAL~~
On 30 Oct 1980
                                ~~TOP SECRET~~

GROUP 3
DOWNGRADING AT 12-YEAR INTERVALS
NOT AUTOMATICALLY DECLASSIFIED   2   ~~TOP SECRET~~ - RESTRICTED DATA
DOD DIR 4200.10

COPY 1 OF 14 COPIES   ~~TOP SECRET~~
                                        Attachment (1) to
                                        SecNav Cont. No. TS-482 JAG CNA-17-69

submarines.

4. (C) With respect to Recommendation 5 of the Report which proposes that operational commanders appropriately consider all information available on navigational hazards and aids when prescribing routes for submarine transits, it is deemed desirable to point out that Commander Submarine Force, U. S. Atlantic Fleet has instituted such a procedure which requires that the tracks of all submarines under the operational control of Commander Submarine Force, U. S. Atlantic Fleet are plotted on bottom contour charts which are maintained in a fully up-to-date status and in addition thereto, all commands having authority to direct submarine movements are instructed to ensure similar care in selecting submarine routing and speeds of advance. Additionally, a complete set of all available bottom contour charts is being established as normal allowance for all submarines and submarine operating authorities.

5. (FOUO) With respect to Recommendation 7 of the Report which suggests establishing a policy preventing persons who are disqualified for psychiatric reasons from again serving on submarines, it is considered that BUMED Manual, Chapter 15, paragraph 15-29(2)(a) adequately protects the best interests of the Navy in this regard. It is appropriate and considered necessary that individuals who have been disqualified for submarine duty for psychiatric reasons of a permanent nature, such as claustrophobic tendencies, unhealthy motivations or difficulties in inter-personal relationships should not be subsequently allowed to serve in submarines. However, individuals who are disqualified for submarine duty for psychiatric reasons of a temporary nature may be requalified but must be re-evaluated by a qualified submarine medical officer who submits his findings and recommendations to the Force Medical Officer who, in turn, makes recommendations to the Submarine Force Commander.

6. (FOUO) The Commander in Chief U. S. Atlantic Fleet specifically concurs in Recommendation 8 of the Report and present policy is being amended to require that all Commanding Officers of submarines should be sent to Prospective Commanding Officer School at least within the two-year period immediately preceding assignment to duty as the Commanding Officer of a submarine. Additionally in this connection, it is recommended that a systematic review and monitoring of the quality of the Prospective Commanding Officer training be continuously conducted. This recommendation is considered to include not only classroom training, but underway shipboard training which will entail the assignment of additional auxiliary submarines for this purpose.

3

TOP SECRET RESTRICTED DATA

7. (TS) It is noted that the testimony of the Polaris Intelligence
Support Officer which appears on Pages 782 through 788 of the
Report of the Court of Inquiry should be reclassified as TOP SECRET
due to its "all source" origin. Accordingly, the pages indicated
in this paragraph are being reclassified as TOP SECRET and are
being transferred from Volume 3 of 10 Volumes to Annex A of the
Report.

8. (TS) Although the precise manner in which the USS SCORPION
(SSN 589) was lost is not known.

Therefore, the importance of strict adherence at all levels of
command to safety precautions cannot be over-emphasized. All hands
are constrained at all times and in all places to learn and practice
the safest manner in which the assigned tasks can be accomplished.
At no time should expediency override safety or common sense. It
should be the unswerving desire of all members of the Naval Service
at all echelons of command to make it their personal way of life to
perform each assigned task, whether it be weapons handling, ship
handling, navigation, fire control, aircraft launching, etc. with
continuous emphasis on the need for safety.

9. (TS) The significant contribution of the Technical Advisory
Group to this Inquiry is recognized and acknowledged. The assistance
of this group provided the primary basis for the working hypothesis
upon which the Court based its opinion of the most probable cause of
the loss of the SCORPION and upon which other possible causes could
be evaluated. It served greatly to clarify the thinking with respect
to this tragedy. An awareness needs to be held, however, that the
probabilities in this case may still have various degrees of remote-
ness and the Commander in Chief U. S. Atlantic Fleet is constrained
to commend caution against total commitment to any particular
scenario postulated herein. Two features do emerge, nevertheless,
in which a very high degree of confidence can be held:

10. (U) Separate action is being initiated by the Commander in
Chief U. S. Atlantic Fleet to appropriately recognize the outstanding performance of duty of the Members of the Court of Inquiry as
well as other personnel associated with the Court.

ANNEX ECLAIR MST - 1964

TOP SECRET - RESTRICTED DATA

11.   (U) Subject to the foregoing, the proceedings, findings of fact, opinions and recommendations contained in the Record of Proceedings of the Court of Inquiry are approved.

Copy to:
CNO (complete)
CINCPACFLT (complete)
COMSUBPAC (complete)
COMSUBLANT (complete)
SUBSAFECEN

INDEX OF WITNESSES

All witnesses called were witnesses for the court.

UNCLASSIFIED

NAME/TITLE	PAGE

Mister ⊦   Civilian   576, 764
Naval Ship Engineering Center

Lieutenant Commandei   , U. S. Navy   586, 916, 10⁞
Navigation Officer, Commander Submarine Force, U. S. Atlantic Fleet

Lieutenant   , Medical Corps, U. S. Navy   605
Medical Officer, Commander Submarine Squadron SIX

Rear Admiral   U. S. Navy   610
Commander Submarine Flotilla SIX

Commander   U. S. Navy   627
USS TAUTOG (SSN 639)

Mister   , Civilian   645
Electric Boat, Division of General Dynamics

Commander   U. S. Navy   665
Operations Officer, Commander Submarine Flotilla EIGHT

Commander .   , U. S. Navy   679
Plans Officer, Commander Carrier Division 20

Lieutenant Commander   ., U. S. Navy   699
Office of the Secretary of Defense, Systems Analyst

Commander   U. S. Navy   709
Headquarters, Material Command, Washington, D. C.

Commander   , U. S. Navy   736
Naval Ship Systems Command, Submarine Branch

Mister   Civilian   750, 806
Code 6165c, Naval Ships Engineering Center, Washington, D. C.

Captain   U. S. Navy   773
Deputy Chief of Staff for Plans and Operation, Commander Submarine
Force, U. S. Atlantic Fleet

Lieutenant (junior grade)   U. S. Navy   777
Auxiliary Division Officer, USS SHARK (SSN 591)

Lieutenant Commander   U. S. Navy   781
Intelligence, Commander in Chief, U. S. Atlantic Fleet

Lieutenant   , U. S. Navy   788
Intelligence, Commander in Chief, U. S. Atlantic Fleet

Lieutenant   --   , U. S. Navy   792
Engineering Officer, USS SHARK (SSN 591)

Lieutenant   U. S. Navy   802, 950
Weapons Officer, Commander Submarine Squadron SIX

Captain   , S. Navy   825
Director, Torpedo Division Naval Ordnance Systems Command

On reconvening in November, after SCORPION was located, the Court focused its attention on "what is" as opposed to "what might have been." While mindful of earlier evidence, a conscious effort was made to prevent undue influence by old concepts and preconceived notions in a search for the most probable cause of the tragedy. Emphasis was placed on complete familiarity with all photographic evidence. Close coordination was maintained with the Naval Research Laboratory Evaluation Group in order to focus the scientific expertise of its members on areas of greatest productivity. The end result has been a greater depth of study than might otherwise have been possible in the time allotted. The Court reviewed its original report in the light of new evidence and has concluded that all findings of fact, opinions, and recommendations previously submitted are still valid except that part of fact number 29 which relates to the identification of an uncharted sunken hull discovered by PARGO during the initial search. Further investigation has identified the sunken hull to be a small merchant ship, not a World War II type submarine as previously identified.

The Court, after inquiring into all additional facts and circumstances connected with the loss of SCORPION, having considered the new evidence and having reconsidered the previous evidence, finds additionally as follows and submits the following supplementary opinions and recommendations:

FINDINGS OF FACT

(S)
(U)

1. That the acoustic signals attributed to SCORPION were recorded at hydroacoustic stations in Argentia, Newfoundland and the Canary Islands. Individual acoustic signals and stations recording them are outlined on the next page entitled "Table of Factual Data - Acoustic Events."

(S)   2. [That acoustic event number one has been determined by experts to be the result of a high energy release, rich in low frequencies with no discernable harmonic structure.]

(S)   3. [That the Technical Director, *B1* testified that the first SCORPION acoustic event looked different and sounded different from subsequent events, but he was unable to determine whether the initial event was an explosion or an implosion.]

(S)   4. [That, in the opinion of experts, SCORPION acoustic events six, seven and eight appear to be from similar sources as indicated by their relative spectra and strong harmonic frequencies *B1*

(S)   5. [That the Director of Research, Naval Research Laboratory, after analyzing available acoustic data, indicated that SCORPION acoustic events one, three, four, five, six, seven, eight, nine, and 13 were probably true events, and events two, 10, 12, and 15 were probably multi-path echos of events one, eight, nine, and 13 respectively, reflected from Plato Sea Mount. He further stated he had not completed his analysis of event 11 and that event 14 was possibly a longer range reflection of event one.]

(U)   6. [That when an explosion occurs in water and does not vent, a bubble is formed that pulses. The size of the charge and the depth of the detonation can be correlated with the frequency of the bubble pulsation.]

(C)   7. That a contact explosion of a charge of about [*B1*] on the outside of a submerged submarine hull, would instantly rupture the pressure hull and create a hole equivalent to several feet in diameter.

(S)   8. That recent experiments conducted by the Naval Ordnance Laboratory and further testimony by experts in underwater explosive effects confirmed that it is possible to detonate an explosive device against a submerged air filled container or a submarine without observing a bubble pulse.]

(C)   9. That the implosion of internal tankage due to hydrostatic pressure may or may not result in the detection of a bubble pulse.

(S)   10. [That a series of calibration shots was conducted in the vicinity of *B1* W approximately one month after the loss of SCORPION, and attempts were made to record these signals at hydro-acoustic stations that recorded the acoustic events attributed to SCORPION. The results are summarized as follows:]

Summary of Calibration Results

Size Charge in lbs TNT	Total # of Shots	Planned Depth in feet	Computed Depth Range in feet	Stations Receiving Results			Remarks
				Canarys	Argentia *B1*	Argentia *B1*	
1.8	9	60	Not given	Very Small			Not used in analysis of propagation path (Supp. Ex. 32)
1.8	7	800	609-817	Yes			
20	5	60	46-57	Yes			
20	13	800	757-847	Yes			
40	1	800	797	Yes			Actual detonation equivalent to 30 lbs TNT
70	2	60	50	Yes			
70	3	1000	547-782	Yes			*Possibly one signal recorded at a very low level
70	3	1500	1507-1598	Yes			
70	5	2000	1917-2142	Yes		*B1*	
70	3	3000	2967-3177	Yes			

(S) 11. That the purpose of the calibration series was to verify predicted sound velocities in order to improve the accuracy of the search datum fix. In addition, the calibration series provided raw data concerning signal strengths and characteristics of known charges detonated at various depths for comparison with acoustic signals attributed to SCORPION.

(S) 12. That the acoustical data which was considered to relate to the sinking of SCORPION was refined and a position determined at *B1* which was designated as Point Oscar.

(S) 13. That the calibration shots fired at 1500 feet were recorded indicating similar energy levels at *B1* at Argentia. The first SCORPION event was recorded at Argentia *B1*

(S) 14. That an attempt was made to determine the depth of the initial SCORPION acoustic event by comparing the shape of the acoustic signal envelope with the envelopes of signals from calibration charges exploded at known depths. Due to the many variables involved, the results were inconclusive.

(S) 15. That the weight of expert testimony, based on a comparison of data from analysis of the SCORPION acoustic events and the calibration series, indicated that the first SCORPION event was either very small (which is not compatable with the recording at the Canary Islands) or it was at 500-700 feet or less.

(S) 16. That the Director of Research, Naval Research Laboratory, stated that by measuring the time difference of two vertical multi-paths of SCORPION acoustic signal number one, he estimated the signal depth to be 400 plus or minus 150 feet.

(S) 17. That expert witnesses concluded that one of the strongest factors indicating that the initial SCORPION acoustic event was at a shallow depth is the requirement to reconcile hydrodynamic considerations with the 91 second delay between the first and second true acoustic events emanating from SCORPION. This consideration is independent of the analysis of acoustic events.

(C)(U) 18. That during the months of August and September an "artifacts field" was discovered to the south and east of Point Oscar. Individual pieces numbered about 50, and were distributed in a random pattern up to two miles from Point Oscar. None of the artifacts, with certainty, could be associated with a submarine.

(U) 19. That at about 0300Z on 30 October 1968, while viewing films on board USNS MIZAR, Captain ▓▓ USN, Commander Submarine Squadron TEN and Commander Task Unit 42.2.1 (Senior Officer, Search Force) detected what he considered to be, and what was later identified as, portions of SCORPION's hull.

(U) 20. That, after determining that the films showed portions of a submarine hull, the Senior Officer, Search Force impounded that film and all subsequently exposed films and retained them in his custody until he delivered them to the appropriate naval authority.

(U) 21. That the depth of water at the position at which SCORPION was found was determined to be 11,100 feet, and the minimum depth of water in the general vicinity was 9,600 feet.

(U) 22. That the bottom where SCORPION rests is level except where disturbed by the impact of the hull. The sediment is clayey silt and a core sample showed globigerina throughout the sample. (Supp. Ex. 40.)

(U) 23. That during June and October in the vicinity of ▓▓ the Senior Officer, Search Force observed variable southerly surface currents at a velocity of .3 to .7 knots. The currents at the bottom are classified as insignificant by the Naval Oceanographic Office.

(S) 24. That the major wreckage of a submarine was found in an area of about 600 feet diameter centered at position [B1] and that this wreckage has been identified as that of SCORPION by the Commander Submarine Force, U. S. Atlantic Fleet and other competent authorities.

(M) 25. That the distribution of debris is probably not fully defined but based on the plot prepared by the Senior Officer, Search Force from photographic and navigational data, the debris field extends for about 3,000 feet in a northwest-southeast direction from the present location of the after hull section. The width of the field is about 1,800 feet.

(M) 26. That, based on the photographic evidence presented to the Court and the evaluation and reports of technical experts on this same photographic evidence, the conditions of the major sections of SCORPION's hull are summarized as follows:

I. After Hull Section

  a. The forward portion of the Engine Room is imploded, collapsed, and/or telescoped into or around the Auxiliary Machinery Space.

  b. There is a clean, circumferential break of the Engine Room at or near the cone cylinder juncture, frame 67.

  c. The tail section, with upper rudder and port control surfaces attached, is visible from about frame 87 to the end of structure, about frame 101, and appears structurally undistorted.

  d. The propellor, with shaft attached, is separated from and located well clear of hull sections.

  e. The light tank plating and framing around the Auxiliary Machinery Space appear to be relatively undamaged.

  f. The visible portion of the forward end of the after hull section terminates at about frame 58 in an apparently clean circumferential fracture.

II. Forward Hull Section

  a. The forward hull portion extends from the extreme bow or forward perpendicular to about frame 29 or 30 on the starboard side. The after edge break appears irregular rather than circumferential. It appears to progress around the heavy periscope and mast insert area on the top centerline at about frame 31 to 32 and then to angle aft to about frame 34 on the port side.

  b. From about frame 26 forward the axis of the bow structure is straight but the remaining structure aft of frame 26 is bent to port about 15°

c. The forward escape trunk upper access hatch is detached.

d. The Bridge Fairwater (Sail) is separated from the hull sections.

e. The outer hull plating between frames 22 and 27 is distorted primarily on the port side with one distorted area on the starboard side about frame 25.

III. Missing Hull Section

A large segment of pressure hull from about frame 38 to frame 34 port and from about frame 38 to frame 29-30 starboard has not been identified in the photographic evidence available.

IV. Bridge Fairwater (Sail)

a. It is lying on its port side separated from the hull sections.

b. The leading edge, top and after edge, above the level of the fairwater planes, exhibit no structural damage.

c. The starboard fairwater plane appears to be undamaged and in normal position.

d. The sail plane access door appears normal but the deck access door is detached.

e. The leading edge of the fairwater below the top of the deck access door is displaced aft and/or to port.

f. The Bridge clamshell appears to be rigged for dive.

g. The fairing for No. two periscope is extended and the upper section (deplumer) is missing.

h. The VLF loop antenna (football) appears undamaged and extended in normal position.

i. The AN/BRA-9 helical antenna is extended, distorted and the fairing missing.

(S) (U) 27. That photographic evidence depicts disturbed bottom areas with large unidentifiable items that appear to be portions of hull structure separated from the major hull sections. (Supp. Ex. 34, 35.)

(U) 28. That Gamma radiation readings, taken at the ocean floor and of a bottom core sample taken at SCORPION's location, gave only normal background readings. Water samples taken in close proximity to the Reactor Compartment of SCORPION gave only normal background readings.

(S) (U) 29. That the Court studied photographic evidence of THRESHER remains and evaluations of implosion testing of U. S. and British submarines.

(C) 30. That the estimated collapse depths for SCORPION's principal pressure hull compartments, tanks, trunks, and bulkheads are as follows:

ITEM	BEST ESTIMATED COLLAPSE DEPTH
Reactor Compartment, forward bulkhead, frame 44	
Reactor Compartment, after bulkhead, frame 52	
Torpedo Room bulkhead, frame 26	
Engine Room bulkhead, frame 64	
Lower hatches to escape trunks and bridge access trunk, pressurized from inside the ship	
Sanitary tank No. 3	
Forward escape trunk	
Torpedo Room pressure hull, frames 13-26	
Operations Compartment pressure hull, frames 26-44 .	
Reactor Compartment pressure hull, frames 44-52	
Auxiliary Machinery Space pressure hull, frames 52-64 .	
Engine Room pressure hull, frames 64-92	
After escape trunk	
After trim tank	
Torpedo tubes	
After closure bulkhead, frames 92-94	
Sanitary tanks No. 1 and No. 2	
Negative tank	
Forward trim tank.	
Auxiliary tanks No. 1 and No. 2	
Forward closure bulkhead, frames 12-13	
WRT tank	
Messenger Buoys	
Bridge access trunk	
HP Air & Oxygen Flasks	

UNCLASSIFIED

(C) (U) 31. That the photographic evidence does not portray, in the evaluation of the structural experts, any of the failure conditions expected or previously experienced in the hydrostatic collapse (implosion) of submarine hull structures.

(S)(U) 32. [That the testimony of experts indicates that the telescoping of the Engine Room forward would be a high energy event, would occur in a fraction of a second and a bubble pulse may or may not be detected.]

(S)(U) 33. That evidence presented did not establish that there was or that there necessarily should be visible evidence of burning or scorching.

(U) 34. That there is no evidence that the loss of SCORPION was the result of an unfriendly act.

(C) (U) 35. That it is probable that the high order detonation of a torpedo in the Torpedo Room would cause sympathetic detonation of other torpedo warheads stowed in the near vicinity.

(U) (FOUO) 36. That, during an oxygen fire in the stern room of USS SARGO (SSN-583) on 14 June 1960, two MK 37 torpedo warheads detonated low order. The pressure hull of SARGO was not ruptured.

(C)(U) 37. That, in the opinion of expert witnesses, the high order detonation of one or more torpedoes in the Torpedo Room could destroy or severely damage the Torpedo Room bulkhead, frame 26, and could damage the surrounding hull structure.

(C) (U) 38. That, in the opinion of the structural experts, the hydrostatic collapse of the Operations Compartment would damage or destroy structure in the vicinity of the forward conical transition section, frames 26 to 28.

(C) (U) 39. That an explosive shock loading in the vicinity of the Operations Compartment would be expected to cause longitudinal whipping of the hull which could induce high bending moment stress in the vicinity of the cone cylinder juncture, frame 67.

(C)(U) 40. That the configuration of the cone cylinder juncture at frame 67 makes this a high stress point due to normal hydrostatic loading and that this area is constrained by the applied stresses to compress less than sections forward or aft of the juncture point.

(C) 41. That the hydrostatic collapse of the Engine Room bulkhead due to flooding forward of frame 64 would probably occur at about an [61] foot pressure head; that such a failure into the Engine Room would, through the bulkhead stiffening and main girder reinforcements, induce additional large bending stresses in the cone cylinder juncture, frame 67; and that the stress loading would tend to force the cone cylinder juncture outward relative to the plating aft of frame 67.

UNCLASSIFIED

(S)   42.   [That the Chief Scientist for the Navy's Strategic Systems Project and Deep Submergence Systems Project testified that it was his opinion, /B/   that an intact submarine which passes through collapse depth will produce one very large complicated, multiple bubble pulse type signal and that there would not be a large number of other major events associated with that collapse. He further testified that the large number of acoustic signals associated with SCORPION is characteristic of the signals from a submarine going through deep depths after experiencing substantial flooding. He therefore concluded that the first SCORPION event was not the type of signal associated with an intact submarine passsing through collapse depth.]

(S)   43.   That the Commander Submarine Force, U. S. Atlantic Fleet has postu-lated that SCORPION was lost as a result of a flooding type casualty which originated at a depth of /B/ feet or less; that for undeter-mined reasons the flooding caused the ship to sink near or beyond the hull designed collapse depth; that the Engine Room telescoped into or around the Auxiliary Machinery Space at a depth of about /B/ feet; and, that this was the initial acoustic event].

(S)(U)   44.   That the Technical Director, NRL, estimated the average sinking rate [between acoustic event one and acoustic event six] to be in excess of 16 feet per second.

(S)   45.   [That NSRDC Report, S-301-H-01 of October 1968, predicted for SCORPION, fully flooded and intact, an impact trajectory velocity of about 35 knots (58+ feet per second) at a depth of 11,000 feet based on the initial conditions of /B/ oot depth, trajectory velocity /B/ knots, full rise on fairwater and stern planes, a three degree down pitch angle, and a rate of change of depth of 22 feet per second.]

(S)(U)   46.   That the Chief Scientist of the Navy's Strategic Systems Project and Deep Submergence Systems Project testified that in his opinion SCORPION probably did not break apart prior to impact with the bottom.

(U)   47.   That the Court attempted to utilize the ship motion simulator facil-ities at the Naval Ships Research and Development Center (NSRDC) to provide the Court with evaluation and guidance indices of possible actions and events associated with SCORPION's loss but was unable to obtain such studies.

(U)   48.   That, following the finding of SCORPION, an evaluation group was established by the Chief of Naval Operations at the Naval Research Laboratory (NRL). The membership of this group was drawn from naval activities which had the diverse scientific and technical competence considered essential to the effective analysis of the available data. (Supp. Ex. 25)

(FOUO)(U) 49. That the NRL Evaluation Group did not, as a group, attempt to make conjecture regarding the cause for the loss of SCORPION.

(C)(U) 50. That an officer who had served in a sister ship of SCORPION and who had been Ship Superintendent for SCORPION during two shipyard availabilities (1965 and 1967) assisted the NRL Evaluation Group in the identification of debris. In testimony before the Court he reduced his level of confidence about identification of some of the parts. Specifically, he expressed doubt about his identification of a torpedo handling track from the Torpedo Room, which is Annotation number one on Supplementary Exhibit 28, and stated that items from other than the Operations Compartment did not seem to be present.

(U)(FOUO) 51. That the identified debris from inside the ship is associated with the Operations Compartment.

(C)(U) 52. There are no objects identified in the debris field which can be definitely associated with the Torpedo Room.

(U) 53. That neither the Senior Officer, Search Force, nor any of the numerous experts who viewed the photographic evidence could identify any object as being from a ship other than SCORPION.

(C)(U) 54. That the twisted pipe-like object bent forward and to starboard from the aftermost portion of the bow section is identified in Supplementary Exhibit 26 as number two periscope. This item appears to have a flange on the end which does not exist on a periscope but is present on the mast of the AN/BPS-9 radar.

(U)(FOUO) 55. That the arrangement of the principle parts of SCORPION, as shown by the photographic mosaic (Supp. Ex. 26), is in general agreement with the plot made by the Senior Officer, Search Force, based on the navigational track of the towed sled. (Supp. Ex. 22).

(U)(FOUO) 56. That the Cartographer who prepared the photographic mosaic expressed doubt about the aspect of the bow section. He stated that the scale of the mosaic was arrived at arbitrarily, is not the same for all parts, and consequently introduces visual distortions.

OPINIONS

(U) The finding of SCORPION's hull does not lessen the tragedy of her loss nor does it lessen the obligation to identify and correct any practice, condition, or deficiency subject to correction.

(U) The photographic evidence made available, on finding SCORPION, reduced areas of speculation regarding the cause of her loss and provided impetus to refocused scientific analysis of all available data pertaining to this tragedy. After careful weighing of all resulting evidence the Court finds that there is still no incontrovertible proof of the exact cause or causes for SCORPION's loss.

(S) 1. That the submarine located on the bottom at *B/* is SCORPION.

(S)(C) 2. That, having weighed all new evidence and having reexamined all previous evidence in the light thereof, the following key facts and technical opinions are considered cardinal in estimating the most probable scenario for the loss of SCORPION. These are:

    a. The first acoustic event

        (1) Originated at a depth of   feet or less;

        (2) *B/*

        (3) Had no bubble pulse frequency recorded.

    b. The casualty, which initiated the first acoustic event

        (1) Represented an incident that was cataclysmic in nature;

        (2) Occurred forward of frame 44; and

        (3) Resulted in uncontrollable flooding.

    c. There is a 91 second time interval between the first acoustic event and the next true acoustic event (Event No. 3).

    d. The remaining true acoustic events, 4 through 13, were recorded over a time span of 74 seconds.

    e. The Engine Room, at about frame 67, telescoped into or around the Auxiliary Machinery Space.

    f. The pressure hull structure between about frames 29 to 38 has been destroyed.

    g. The visible hull plating of the remaining hull sections show an absence of massive damage thereto.

(8) (C) 3. That the following is a logical general scenario related to the
(5)   [acoustic events:]

a. Ship is at a depth of 250 feet or less. Position of watertight
    doors open if normal cruising, shut if in an emergency situation.
    Casualty occurs which results in flooding from sea [Acoustic
    Event #1)] If not incapacitated, personnel initiate recovery
    action, but in any event, ship begins to lose depth control due
    to inability to control or counteract flooding.

b. The flooding most probably occurred as a result of a casualty
    in the area of the Operations Compartment or Torpedo Room.

    (1) If the initial casualty was in the area of the Operations
        Compartment, on reaching a depth of [B/] feet the Reactor
        Compartment bulkheads rupture. If the tunnel doors were shut,
        the forward and after bulkheads collapse in quick succession.
        If open, the Reactor Compartment below the tunnel ruptures.
        The Torpedo Room may or may not flood during this period
        depending on the nature of the initial casualty and whether
        the Torpedo Room watertight door was open or shut.

    (2) If the initial casualty was in the area of the Torpedo Room,
        extent of flooding would depend on whether the Torpedo Room
        bulkhead was damaged and whether the watertight door was open
        or shut.

c. The Engine Room door would probably now be shut whether or not it
    was shut before the flooding casualty occurred.

d. On reaching a depth of [B/] feet:

    (1) If the initial casualty was in the area of the Operations
        Compartment and if the Torpedo Room door had been shut, the
        Torpedo Room bulkhead collapses into the Torpedo Room and the
        forward escape hatches blow out.

    (2) If the initial casualty was in the Torpedo Room, and the
        bulkhead had not previously been ruptured and the door had been
        shut, the Torpedo Room bulkhead now collapses into the
        Operations Compartment and the forward escape trunk hatches
        blow out.

    (3) If the bulkhead had been previously ruptured or weakened, it
        could have collapsed at a lesser depth.

    (4) [In any event, a bubble pulse results from this bulkhead collapse
        or escape trunk blow-out (Acoustic Event #3).]

e. Shortly after the above event, due to a combined sea and air pressure
    in the Auxiliary Machinery Space now equal to about [B/] feet of
    water, the Engine Room bulkhead collapses into the Engine Room. This
    results in telescoping of the Engine Room into the Auxiliary Machinery
    Space [Acoustic Event #4] This piston effect, driving forward against
    what is now a considerable volume of water in the ship forward of the
    Engine Room bulkhead, could have resulted in further severe damage and
    rupture to the Operations Compartment hull plating. The main shaft is
    probably extruded at this time but remains attached to the ship.

f. Ship is now completely flooded except for various hard tanks and air pockets and continues to sink rapidly in excess of 15 feet per second. On passing approximately _B/_ feet, an internal tank implodes (Acoustic Event #5).

g. On passing _B/_ feet, torpedo tubes or other tankage implode in fairly rapid succession (Acoustic Events #6, #7, and #8).

h. As SCORPION continues to sink below _B/_ feet, remaining true acoustic events can logically be accounted for as follows:

> Event #9 (a multiple event) - Internal tankage.
>
> Event #11 - Messenger buoy(s).
>
> Events #13-14 - Internal tankage.

i. Ship, still in one piece although severly damaged amidships, continues to sink, reaching a trajectory velocity of approximately 25-35 knots. Ship hits the bottom with a relatively small trim angle.

j. On impact, the ship breaks apart. The sail is probably separated from the ship at this time. The main sections of the hull probably bounce and skip before coming to their final resting place. A considerable amount of debris is spilled out during this process. The main shaft, either on initial impact or shortly thereafter, is thrown clear with screw still attached. The bow section plows deeply into the bottom in an upright position. The stern section slews around and finally comes to rest on its starboard side. During this movement, or perhaps on initial impact with the bottom, the starboard stabilizer and stern plane snap off, separate, and are thrown clear.

k. The pressure/depth ranges stated above reflect considerations to account for flooding rates, damage conditions, and dynamics of ship motion.

4. That in addition to the cardinal points considered in construction of the above scenario, the following facts and opinions are pertinent in support of a most likely cause of the loss of SCORPION:

(U) a. The initial casualty, which resulted in flooding, was most probably due to causes other than characteristic implosion of a major compartment.

(U) b. The visible structural damage in the Operations Compartment does not clearly indicate the failure mode but is more probably associated with an explosion rather than an implosion.

(U) c. If an external explosion in contact with the pressure hull had initiated the casualty, the resulting gas bubble could vent into the submarine and no bubble pulse would be detected.

253

(C) (U)   d. The initial casualty resulted in flooding forward of the center of
          gravity generating a down angle on the ship. By the time of
          telescoping of the Engine Room, it is postulated that this down
          angle could approximate 60°. Subsequent to telescoping and complete
          flooding of the ship, the trim angle would tend to decrease.

(S) (U)   e. [The two signals, 1.8 minutes apart, detected by SOSUS emanated from
          SCORPION and correspond to acoustic events number one and six or
          to event number one and a combination of events five, six, and
          seven.]

(C) (U)   f. The Engine Room was not flooded by [the first event] and was the
          last compartment to flood.

(C) (U)   g. Except for the Engine Room, SCORPION was fully flooded before
          passing hull collapse depth.

(C) (U)   h. The location of the initial casualty and the resultant flooding
          caused the Engine Room bulkhead to collapse into the Engine Room
          initiating failure of the cone cylinder juncture about frame 67.

(S) (U)   i. [Telescoping of the Engine Room into the Auxiliary Machinery Space
          produced a high energy, low frequency acoustic event and may or
          may not have produced a detectable bubble pulse.]

(S) (U)   j. [Telescoping of the Engine Room corresponds most probably to acoustic
          event number four; however, if the Torpedo Room bulkhead was
          destroyed or severely damaged by event number one, the telescoping
          could correspond to event number three.]

(S) (U)   k. [Although the nature and magnitude of acoustic events six, seven
          and eight suggest the Engine Room telescoping, analysis of the depth
          of SCORPION at the times of these events mitigate against this
          conclusion.]

(FOUO) (U) l. The effective pressure applied to internal structures could lag the
          static pressure head due to flooding rates, damage conditions, and
          dynamics of ship motion.

(C)   m. [B1

                                        can affect the signal reception capability
          as evidenced by the B1   calibration shots heard at Argentia
          when detonated at a depth of 1500 feet. B1

          or greater, it could have occurred at about B1

(C) (U)   n. Separation of the hull in the Operations Compartment area occurred
          upon impact with the bottom; however, severe damage to this area
          resulted from the initial casualty and was aggravated by the
          telescoping of the Engine Room and the action of hydrodynamic
          forces while sinking.

(C) (U)   o. The detachment of the propellor and shaft was not an initiating
          casualty.

(U) (S) 5. [That the finding of SCORPION so close to the point computed from the acoustic events leaves no doubt that these events did in fact emanate from SCORPION.]

(U) (FOUO) 6. That currents in the area would have a limited effect on the distribution of debris, but light objects, dropped from near the surface, would probably be carried in a southerly direction.

(U) 7. That all photographs available at this time, which pertain to the loss of SCORPION, have been examined to discover and analyze any clues which might lead to an explanation for the loss of SCORPION.

(U) (FOUO) 8. That no definitely identifiable human remains appeared in any photograph reviewed by the Court.

(U) (S) 9. [An examination of the photographs of SCORPION's hull and associated debris does not lead to the certain conclusion that the first acoustic event was caused by either an explosion or an implosion.]

(U) (C) 10. That the fact that SCORPION was limited to an operating depth of ⟨B⟩ feet, though designed for a test depth of ⟨B⟩ feet, supports the conclusion that she was above ⟨B⟩ feet when the initial casualty occurred.

(S) (U) 11. That the positions of the various masts, relative to the top of the Bridge Fairwater, do not permit a certain conclusion as to mode of operations or depth of the ship at the time of the initial casualty.

(U) (S) 12. [That acoustic event number one was most probably an explosion of large charge weight external to the pressure hull.]

(U) (S) 13. [That the initial acoustic event produced a degree of damage and rate of flooding from which no submarine could be expected to survive.]

(S) (U) 14. That, as established in the original report (Fact 271), the only items on board, forward of frame 44, with sufficient explosive energy to cause the initial event, were the torpedo warheads.

(S) (U) 15. That in view of the lack of identifiable debris from the Torpedo Room, it is concluded that the Torpedo Room was not the location of a major explosive event.

(S) (U) 16. That, while the sequence of events postulated by the Commander Submarine Force, U.S. Atlantic Fleet is considered possible, the weight of evidence leads to the conclusion that such a sequence of events was not probable.

(S) (U) 17. That in the absence of evidence to the contrary it is assumed that objects in the "artifact field" are associated with SCORPION.

(S) (U) 18. That some debris spilled out of the Operations Compartment of SCORPION on her way to the bottom but most of the debris was expelled on impact.

(S) (U) 19. That the absence of air or oxygen flasks in the debris field indicates that there was no severe damage to the ballast tanks in which they are located and supports the opinion that the Engine Room telescoped into rather than around the Auxiliary Machinery Space.

(S) (U) 20. That the identifiable debris does not lead to a determination of the cause for the loss of SCORPION.

(S) (U) 21. That the damage to the stern planes and rudders was not a primary cause of loss of SCORPION.

(S) (U) 22. That there is no conclusive photographic evidence that relates the condition or position of the visible ship control surfaces to the cause for the loss of SCORPION.

(S) (U) 23. That the lower trunk access hatches could fail catastrophically from pressure inside the submarine and the resultant water jet could detach or destroy the upper hatches.

(S) (U) 24. That, since the Bridge Fairwater appears essentially undamaged in the vicinity of the bridge access trunk, implosion or collapse of the bridge access trunk is improbable.

(S) (U) 25. That the Bridge Fairwater was probably loosened by the initial event and separated from the ship on impact with the bottom.

(S) (U) 26. That the outer hull distortion about frames 22 to 27 port most probably resulted from the hydrodynamic forces attendant to sinking and from impact on the bottom.

(S) (U) 27. That the outer hull damage about frame 25 starboard is most probably a wrinkle due to distortion from sinking motions or bottom impact.

(C) (U) 28. That the visible structural failures shown in the photographs are not indicative of deficient or defective materials or workmanship as a primary cause of SCORPION's loss.

(U) (FOUO) 29. That the information sought from the NSRDC ship motion simulator studies has been adduced by other means and the lack of these studies does not adversely affect the findings of the Court.

(U)   30. That the additional evidence supports the finding that no radiological hazard resulted from the loss of SCORPION.

(U)   31. That the additional evidence does not establish that the loss of SCORPION and deaths of those embarked were caused by the intent, fault, negligence, or inefficiency of any person or persons in the naval service or connected therewith.

RECOMMENDATIONS

1. That, as part of the continuing efforts to obtain additional clues as to the cause for this tragedy and to prevent others, a further examination of the main hull sections of SCORPION and the associated debris field be conducted as and when practicable using the latest techniques available.

2. That consideration be given to the research and study of large weight contact explosions to determine the damage mechanism, to evaluate secondary effects thereof and to provide currently unavailable data for future design improvements for damage resistance to high performance submarines.

Vice Admiral, U.S. Navy (Retired)
President

Rear Admiral, U.S. Navy
Member

Captain, U.S. Navy
Member

Captain, U.S. Navy
Member

Captain, U.S. Navy
Member

Captain, U.S. Navy
Member

Commander, U.S. Navy
Member

Fina

Vice Admiral, U.S. Navy (Retired)
President

Captain, JAGC, U.S. Navy
Counsel for the Court

258

UNCLASSIFIED

~~CONFIDENTIAL~~

The Court, after inquiring into all the facts and circumstances connected with the incident which occasioned the inquiry, and having considered the evidence, finds as follows and submits the following opinions and recommendations:

FINDINGS OF FACT

(U) 1. That the USS SCORPION (SSN589) was built by the Electric Boat Division, General Dynamics Corporation at Groton, Connecticut, the second ship of the SSN588 Class. (Ex 21)

(U) 2. That SCORPION was launched in December 1959 and was commissioned on 29 July 1960. (Ex 21)

(U) 3. That SCORPION's main propulsion plant consisted of a model S5W nuclear power plant.

4. That the design test depth of SCORPION was [$b(1)$] and that the authorized operating depth was [restricted to $b(1)$] by CNO message 041529Z May 1963 and COMSUBLANT/COMSUBPAC Joint Instruction 03120.9A/ 03120.15A.

(U) 5. That SCORPION was a unit of Submarine Division 62 and Submarine Squadron 6 and Norfolk, Virginia was assigned as her homeport.

(U) 6. That SCORPION underwent Post Shakedown Availability from 3 October 1960 to 2 January 1961 at Electric Boat Division. She underwent a Regular Overhaul (RO) from 8 June 1963 to 30 April 1964 at Charleston Naval Shipyard and a Restricted Availability (RAV) for refueling, interim docking, and voyage repairs from 1 February 1967 to 6 October 1967 at Norfolk Naval Shipyard.

(U) 7. That Commander Francis Atwood SLATTERY, U. S. Navy, 584741/1100, took command of SCORPION on 17 October 1967, one day before commencement of refresher training, and five days after reporting on board.

(U) 8. That SCORPION deployed from Norfolk, Virginia, on 15 February 1968, and on her transit to the Mediterranean was in company with Commander Task Group 83.4 (COMCARDIV 20). She was employed in controlled and free play exercises. The Plans Officer, Task Group 83.4, stated that SCORPION earned a good reputation with the Task Group in every facet of her operations.

(U) 9. That SCORPION was moored in vicinity of USS CANOPUS (AS34) in Rota, Spain from 29 February to 5 March 1968. (Ex 21)

(U) 10. That SCORPION made the following port visits while in the Mediterranean:

Taranto, Italy	10-12 March
Augusta Bay, Sicily	23-30 March
Naples, Italy	10-15 April
Naples, Italy	20-28 April

(Ex 21)

UNCLASSIFIED

(U)   11. That SCORPION participated in two NATO exercises and SIXTH Fleet operations while in the Mediterranean. (Ex 21)

(U)   12. That during her deployment in the Mediterranean SCORPION operated essentially throughout her authorized depth and speed range. (Ex 164)

(U)   13. That on the night of 16-17 May 1968, SCORPION rendezvoused with a boat outside the breakwater at Rota, Spain to transfer two men and seven messages. This was SCORPION's last physical contact with shore based activities.

(U)   14. That at 170001Z May 1963 COMSUBLANT assumed direct operational control of SCORPION. (Ex 72)

(C)   15. That on 20 May 1968, SCORPION was assigned a Great Circle Track from [$\rightarrow$ (1)] then via submarine transit lanes to Norfolk with a speed of advance of 18 knots] and was directed to report ETA Norfolk. (Ex 83)

(C)   16. That SCORPION's message 212354Z May 1968 reported her 220001Z posit as [$\rightarrow$ (1)] and gave her ETA at Norfolk as 271700Z. This message was receipted for by U. S. Naval Communication Station, Greece at 220303Z, after having been in communication with SCORPION since 220102Z [$\rightarrow$ (1)] KHZ. (Exs 73 and 123)

(U)   17. That no further communications were received from SCORPION after her 212354Z May 1968 message.

(U)   18. That the operation order under which SCORPION was operating while in transit to Norfolk required electronic silence except as necessary for safety and certain other specified situations.

(U)   19. That between 220001Z and 271700Z May, nine messages were transmitted on the submarine broadcast to SCORPION. Three of these (COMSUBDIV 62 211337Z first transmitted at 230414Z; COMNAVSHIPYD NORVA 212157Z first transmitted about 240400Z; and COMSUBDIV 62 242006Z first transmitted at 250217Z) requested replies from SCORPION. No replies were received.

(U)   20. That the weather along SCORPION's prescribed track from 21 to 27 May was generally good with maximum wind velocity of about 25 knots and maximum sea height about 12 feet.

(U)   21. That at about 271640Z May (1240 local), Commanding Officer, USS ORION (AS18), who was acting Commander Submarine Squadron 6, advised COMSUBLANT that SCORPION had not established communications to obtain her berthing assignment and arrange tug services. COMSUBLANT initiated an intensive communications check with no success.

(U)   22. That at 271915Z May (1515 local) SUBMISS was declared and an intensive air, surface, and subsurface search was initiated.

(U)   23.   That a period of 136 hours elapsed from the time of last communications from SCORPION until the search was initiated at 271915Z May.

(U)   24.   That on 27 May 1968, COMSUBLANT (VADM   , USN) was embarked in USS PARGO (SSN650) out of New London, Connecticut. His administrative headquarters remained in Norfolk, Virginia.

(U)   25.   That when SUBMISS was declared, COMSUBLANT in PARGO proceeded to the vicinity of SCORPION's track at 73°West and assumed the duties as Officer in Charge of Search and Rescue.

(U)   26.   That an extensive air, surface and subsurface search was conducted covering the entire area along SCORPION's track from Norfolk to her last known position. Units initially assigned included 18 destroyer types, 12 submarines, 5 submarine rescue ships, 1 oceanographic survey ship, and 1 fleet oiler. The primary air search consisted of up to 27 flights per day of long range patrol aircraft.

(U)   27.   That the initial search effort was divided into three general areas: the western Atlantic Shelf, the area of SCORPION's last known position, and the broad ocean area in between. Priority, in the bottom search, was given to the western shelf and the sea mount area near SCORPION's last known position since only in these areas was rescue and salvage considered possible. The 2,000 to 3,000 fathom depths in the broad ocean area are in excess of the maximum depth where rescue and salvage is possible.

(U)   28.   That on 29 May, COMSUBLANT returned to his Norfolk headquarters and Commander Submarine Flotilla 6 (RADM   USN) embarked in USS STANDLEY (DLG32) was designated Senior Officer Search Force. COMSUBLANT retained his responsibilities as Officer in Charge of Search and Rescue.

(U)   29.   That the close-in area along SCORPION's track, from 73°West to the 30 fathom curve, was intensively searched by 19 surface ships and 10 submarines with negative results. The effectiveness of this search was indicated by the discovery of a previously uncharted sunken submarine hull by PARGO. Divers identified the submarine as a World War II type, probably German. The probability of detecting SCORPION in this area was estimated by the search force to be 100% if on the surface and 94% if on the bottom.

(U)   30.   That the initial surface search of the broad ocean area was conducted by five surface ships and five submarines transiting in two lines with track spacing varying from five to ten miles depending on visibility and sea conditions. The submarine element trailed the surface element by about 135 miles to ensure daylight coverage of SCORPION's entire track by either the submarine element or the surface element. The probability of detecting SCORPION if she were disabled on the surface in the area searched was estimated by the search force to be 96% to 99%.

(U) 31. That the search probability of detection in the broad ocean area was increased by the participation of at least 12 additional surface ships and submarines diverted from normal transits in order to enhance the total search effort. The above includes the [French submarine REQUIN] which participated during the period 2-4 June.

(U) 32. That aircraft searched the area 20 miles on either side of SCORPION's track from her last known position to Norfolk. The area west of 60°W was expanded to 40 miles either side.

(U) 33. That in the opinion of Commander Antisubmarine Warfare Force Atlantic, the air search effort was 97.5% to 99.9% effective. He further stated that, "Had any visible or otherwise detectable 'sign' of SCORPION manifested itself at or near the surface. . .the chances of an air detection would be in the evaluation range of 'high probable' to 'certain' contact."

(U) 34. That the area of Cruiser Sea Mount and Hyeres Bank was searched initially by two submarines and two submarine rescue ships. This was followed by a detailed bathymetric survey by USS COMPASS ISLAND (AG153).

(U) 35. That the probability of detecting SCORPION in the sea mount area was estimated by the search force to be 100% if surfaced, 98% is resting on top of Cruiser Sea Mount, and 97% if bottomed on Hyeres Bank. The possibility of detecting SCORPION if bottomed in the rest of the area was considered remote due to the generally rugged terrain and steep slopes.

(U) 36. That two deep diving vehicles were positioned in the Azores for possible use in the sea mount area.

(U) 37. That USNS MIZAR arrived in the area on 12 June to conduct a detailed bottom search using a magnetometer, ocean bottom scanning sonar (OBSS) and a camera, all mounted on a towed sled.

(U) 38. That a review of available intelligence was conducted by CINCLANTFLT to determine if information was available that might relate in any way to the loss of SCORPION.

(U) 39. That there were no known Soviet or Bloc surface warships, merchant ships, submarines, or aircraft within 200 miles of SCORPION's last reported position during the period she was transmitting (220102Z to 220303Z May).

(U) 40. That two Soviet and one Cuban cargo ship crossed SCORPION's track on 24 May. These were the only known Soviet or Bloc merchant ships to cross SCORPION's track during the period 220001Z to 271700Z. Two of the ships are believed to have passed in excess of 100 miles from SCORPION's PIM. The third ship, the Soviet cargo ship [KASIMOV,] passed approximately 50 miles behind SCORPION's PIM. All three ships crossed SCORPION's track over 24 hours after the acoustic event at 2218447 May

(S) (u)   41.   That no discreet low frequency identifiable information from which to determine SCORPION's mode of operation was recorded on the Canary Island hydrophones.

(S) (u)   42.   That no contact, that could be identified as SCORPION, was held on the Sound Surveillance System Atlantic (SOSUS) at any time after she departed Rota, Spain, on 17 May.

(S)   43.   That in the opinion of Commander Oceanographic Systems Atlantic, the probability of gaining SOSUS contact on SCORPION [↲-(1)
                                                                                        ].

(S) (u)   44.   That no other submarine contacts were held by SOSUS in the vicinity of SCORPION's track around the time of the acoustic event.

(U) (FOUO)   45.   That the Chairman of the Technical Advisory Group (see Fact 55) reported that they recommended that no costly effort be made to search for nuclear contamination in sea water because of the highly unproductive operation during the search for THRESHER. Water sampling was not conducted as a regular part of the SCORPION search effort, however limited sampling was done by STURGEON with no significant results. No radioactivity was detected on any of the flotsam recovered. (Ex 187)

(U) (S)   46.   That a Soviet [hydro-acoustic] operation was being conducted southwest of the Canary Islands during the period of SCORPION's return transit from the Mediterranean. The group consisted of two hydrographic survey ships, a submarine rescue ship, and an [ECHO-II class] nuclear submarine.

(S)   47.   (SEE ANNEX A.)

(S) (u)   48.   That two additional Soviet ships, a KRUPNY class guided missile destroyer and an oiler, departed Algiers about 18 May 1968. They departed the Mediterranean and made a direct transit to join the ships operating southwest of the Canary Islands. They did not arrive in the area until after SCORPION was about 200 miles to the west.

(U) (S)   49.   That two of the Soviet ships in the area were capable of firing surface-to-surface missiles, the [ECHO-II class] submarine [and the KRUPNY class destroyer. There is [no evidence that either vessel fired a missile during the period [220001Z to 271700Z May].

(S) (u)   50.   That U. S. Navy patrol aircraft maintained surveillance coverage of the Soviet forces until 19 May. This coverage was resumed on 21 May. Sightings on 21 May and 22 May, both before and after SCORPION's last position report, placed all units over 200 miles from SCORPION's last known position and in the same general area where they had previously been operating.

(S) (u)   51.   That there were no observed changes in the pattern of operations of the Soviet ships, either before or after SCORPION's loss, that were

(S)(U) 52. That there was no evidence of any other Soviet or Bloc warship within 1,000 miles of SCORPION's general area.

(S)(U) 53. That available intelligence estimates indicate that there was no evidence of any Soviet preparations for hostilities or a crisis situation such as would be expected in the event of a premeditated attack on SCORPION.

(S)(U) 54. That there was no evidence of a nuclear explosion in the Atlantic area during the period 220001Z to 271700Z May.

(U) 55. That a group of experts, including several scientists, assisted the CNO in planning possible rescue and recovery operations. This group was subsequently formally established as a Technical Advisory Group (TAG) with Dr. ____ , Chief Scientist of the Deep Submergence Submarine Project, as chairman.

(S) 56. That the TAG alerted all research and development activities associated with the Deep Submergence Submarine Project and reviewed hydro-acoustic information available [b (1)
    ] and the Navy Oceanographic System, Atlantic.]

(S) 57. That a series of unidentified anomalies or acoustic disturbances was discovered on [b (1)   ] recordings from Argentia, Newfoundland, [b (1)   ] and the Ocean Systems Atlantic recordings from eight different locations.

(S) 58. That the nature of the acoustic events indicated that they were non-seismic in character and were not unlike the series of events recorded during the THRESHER disaster in 1963.

(S) 59. That the approximate time of the acoustic event was 221844Z May. The total event consisted of about 15 pulses occurring in a total time frame of three minutes and ten seconds. Pulse number two occurred 26 seconds and pulse number three occurred one minute 31 seconds after pulse number one. All of the remaining pulses followed in rapid succession, with intervals varying from three to 18 seconds between pulses. (Ex 138)

(S) 60. That a three position fix was obtained on the acoustic events at [b (1)
    b (1)   ]. The fix correlated with SCORPION's most probable track and speed of advance.

(S) 61. That the vicinity of [b (1)   ] was designated an area of special interest by the Chief of Naval Operations on 31 May 1968 (CNO msg 311840Z MAY).

(S) 62. That a bathymetric survey of the area of special interest, [b (1)
    b (1)   ] was conducted by COMPASS ISLAND and a relief model of the ocean floor area was constructed. [In addition, COMPASS ISLAND dropped a series of explosive charges in order to refine datum and gain additional acoustic data for analysis

(U) 63. That when an explosion occurs in water and does not vent, a bubble is formed that pulsates. The size of the charge and the depth of the detonation can be correlated with the frequency of the bubble pulse.

u (C) 64. That the Director of Columbia University's acoustic research station in Bermuda, Mr. B6 , conducted an experiment in which he detonated a small charge in free space underwater and recorded the characteristic bubble pulse. He then detonated a similar charge set against a small can and the explosion vented into the can and no bubble pulse was observed.

(TS) 65. (SEE ANNEX A.)

u (S) 66. That pulse numbers one and two exhibited no harmonic structure that would indicate a bubble pulse frequency. Pulse number three and several subsequent pulses showed definite harmonic structure indicating a bubble pulse frequency.

u (S) 67. That it is the unanimous opinion of all the experts of the TAG who have analyzed the recordings of the 22 May acoustic event in the Atlantic that it emanated from SCORPION.

u (S) 68. That Doctor B6 the TAG Chairman, reported an expert had listened to the tape recording of the initial acoustic event and that "he says that it sounds like an explosion, it looks like an explosion."

u (S) 69. That during the calibration tests conducted by COMPASS ISLAND, with the size of charge constant, the amplitude of the received signal increased as depth increased.

u (S) 70. That the amplitude of the first event of the 22 May acoustic disturbance was greater than the amplitude of a 70-pound charge detonated at 60 feet and less than a 70-pound charge detonated at 1500 feet.

u (S) 71. That in June an object, apparently a piece of metal, was photographed by MIZAR on the ocean floor in the vicinity of [4 (1)
4 (1)] The object was evaluated by the Technical Advisory Group as a piece of twisted metal about two feet long that appears to be shiny, uncorroded and not covered with silt. (Ex.176, photograph #4)

N(u) 72. That on 17 June, Commander Submarine Squadron 12 (Captain B6 USN) relieved Rear Admiral B6 as Senior Officer, Search Force.

(U) 73. That on 30 June, Commander Submarine Squadron 4 (Captain B6 USN) relieved Captain B6 as Senior Officer, Search Force. B6

(U) 74. That, as of the date of this report, the search for SCORPION has been unsuccessful and is continuing.

(U) 75. That SCORPION was declared presumed lost by the Chief of Naval Opera-

UNCLASSIFIED

(U) 76. That in a memorandum of 5 June 1968 from SECNAV to CNO, determination was made, under the provisions of Chapter 10, Title 37 of the U. S. Code, that all personnel aboard SCORPION died on 5 June 1968.

(U) 77. That the following persons were on board SCORPION when she departed Rota, Spain, on 17 May 1968, and were aboard when she was lost:

SLATTERY, Francis Atwood	CDR	USN
LLOYD, David Bennett	LCDR	USN
STEPHENS, Daniel Peter	LCDR	USN
FLESCH, Robert Walter	LT	USN
HARWI, William Clarke	LT	USN
BURKE, John Patrick	LT	USN
FARRIN, George Patrick	LT	USN
LAMBERTH, Charles Lee	LT	USN
SWEET, John Charles	LTJG	USN
SMITH, Laughton Douglas	LTJG	USN
FORRESTER, James Walter, Jr.	LTJG	USN
ODENING, Michael Anthony	LTJG	USN
ALLEN, Keith Alexander Martin	FTG3(SS)	USNR
AMTOWER, Thomas Edward	IC2(SU)	USN
ANNABLE, George Gile	MM2(SU)	USN
BARR, Joseph Anthony, Jr.	FN(SS)	USN
BAILEY, Michael Jon	RM2(SS)	USN
BISHOP, Walter William	TMC(SS)	USN
BLAKE, Michael Reid	IC3(SU)	USN
BLOCKER, Robert Harold	MM1(SS)	USN
BROCKER, Kenneth Ray	MM2(SS)	USN
BRUEGGEMAN, James Kenneth	MM1(SS)	USN
BRYAN, Robert Eugene	MMC(SS)	USN
BURNS, Daniel Paul, Jr.	RMSN(SG)	USNR
BYERS, Ronald Lee	IC2(SS)	USN
CAMPBELL, Duglas Leroy	MM2(SS)	USN
CARDULLO, Samuel "J."	MM3(SS)	USN
CAREY, Francis King	MM2(SS)	USN
CARPENTER, Gary James	SN(SU)	USN
CHANDLER, Robert Lee	MM1(SS)	USN
CHRISTIANSEN, Mark Helton	MM1(SS)	USN
CONSTANTINO, Romeo	SD1(SS)	USN
COWAN, Robert James	MM1(SS)	USN
CROSS, Joseph	SD1(SS)	USN
DENNEY, Garlin Ray	RMC(SS)	USN
DUNN, Michael Edward	FA(SU)	USN
ENGELHART, Richard Philip	ETR2(SU)	USN
FENNICK, William Ralph	FTGSN(SU)	USN
FOLI, Vernon Mark	IC3(SS)	USN
FRANK, Ronald Anthony	SN(SU)	USN
GIBSON, Michael David	CSSN(SS)	USN
GLEASON, Steven Dean	IC2(SD)	USN

HENRY, Michael Edward	STS2(SS)	USN
HESS, Larry Leroy	SK1(SS)	USN
HOGELAND, Richard Curtis	ETR1(SS)	USN
HOUGE, John Richard	MM1(SS)	USN
HUBER, Ralph Robert	EM2(SU)	USN
HUCKELBERRY, Harry David	TM2(SS)	USN
JOHNSON, John Frank	EM3(SU)	USN
JOHNSON, Robert	RMCS(SS)	USN
JOHNSON, Steven Leroy	IC3(SS)	USN
JOHNSTON, Julius III	QM2(SS)	USN
KAHANEK, Patrick Charles	FN(SU)	USN
KARMASEK, Donald Terry	TM2(SS)	USN
KERNTKE, Richard Allen	MMCS(SS)	USN
KIPP, Rodney Joseph	ETR3(SS)	USN
KNAPP, Dennis Charles	MM3(SU)	USN
LANIER, Max Franklin	MM1(SS)	USN
LIVINGSTON, John Weichert	ET1(SS)	USN
MARTIN, Kenneth Robert	ETN2(SU)	USN
MAZZUCHI, Frank Patsy	QMCS(SS)	USN
McGuire, Michael Lee	ET1(SS)	USN
MIKSAD, Steven Charles	TMSN(SU)	USN
MILLER, Joseph Francis, Jr.	TMSN(SU)	USN
MOBLEY, Cecil Frederick	MM2(SS)	USN
MORRISON, Raymond Dale	QM1(SS)	USN
PETERSEN, Daniel Christopher	EMC(SS)	USN
PFERRER, Dennis Paul	QM3(SS)	USN
POSPISIL, Gerald Stanley	EM1(SS)	USN
POWELL, Donald Richard	IC3(SU)	USN
RAY, Earl Lester, Jr.	MM2(SU)	USN
SANTANA, Jorge Luis	CS1(SS)	USN
SAVILLE, Lynn Thompson	HMC(SS)	USN
SCHAFFER, Richard George	ETN2(SS)	USN
SCHOONOVER, William Newman	SN(SU)	USN
SEIFERT, Phillip Allan	SN(SU)	USN
SMITH, George Elmet, Jr.	ETC(SS)	USN
SMITH, Robert Bernard	MM2(SS)	USN
SNAPP, Harold Robert, Jr.	ST1(SS)	USN
STEPHENS, Joel Candler	ETM2(SS)	USN
STONE, David Burton	MM2(SS)	USN
STURGILL, John Phillip	EM2(SU)	USN
SUMMERS, Richard Norman	YN3(SU)	USNR
SWEENEY, John Driscoll, Jr.	TMSN(SG)	USNR
TINDOL, James Frank, III	ETM2(SS)	USN
VEERHUSEN, Johnny Gerald	CSSN(SU)	USN
VIOLETTI, Robert Paul	TM3(SU)	USN
VOSS, Ronald James	ST3(SU)	USN
WALLACE, John Michael	FTG1(SS)	USN
WATKINS, Joel Kurt	MM1(SS)	USN
WATSON, Robert Westley	MMFN(SU)	USN
WEBB, James Edwin	MM2(SU)	USN

(U) 78. That the persons listed as being aboard were military members of the Naval Service on active duty.

(U) 79. That all persons on board SCORPION were on board for the purpose of executing official duties.

(U) 80. That Commander Slattery completed Prospective Commanding Officer School (PCO) in July 1964, at which time he was serving in USS NAUTILUS (SSN571). Subsequently he served as Executive Officer in NAUTILUS for 23 months, and attended the Naval War College. Immediately prior to reporting on board SCORPION he spent three months in PCO training in Naval Reactors.

(U) 81. That the policy of the Commanders, Atlantic/Pacific Submarine Forces is: "An officer ordered to command who has already attended PCO School but has been absent from submarine duty in excess of 24 months will be ordered via PCO School or, if this is not possible, then four weeks temporary duty with the parent squadron."

(U) ~~(FOUO)~~ 82. That Commander Slattery had been absent from submarine duty for 15 months between his 23 month tour as Executive Officer on NAUTILUS (all except three months of which was spent in a Naval Shipyard) and taking command of SCORPION, a faster and more maneuverable ship than those submarines on which he had previously served. His other assignments on board NAUTILUS were:

> Electrical and Reactor Control Officer - 15 months
>
> Main Propulsion Assistant - 5 months
>
> Engineer Officer - 22 months

(U) 83. That Lieutenant Commander David Bennett Lloyd, USN, B-6 relieved as Executive Officer on 5 January 1968. He had completed PCO School in October 1965 and was qualified to command submarines.

(U) 84. That in October 1967, SCORPION began refresher training after her restricted availability and the following numbers of officers and crew members subsequently lost were on board:

> 10 of the 12 officers
>
> 71 of the 87 enlisted men (all of the torpedo "gang" except the leading torpedoman, and all of the fire controlmen)

(U) 85. That SCORPION underwent refresher training at New London, Connecticut, under the supervision of the Submarine School and with COMSUBDIV 62 present and participating, during the period 20-30 October 1967. This training included refresher training in submarine escape procedures.

(U) 86. That, since the loss of THRESHER in 1963, diving trainers and submarine

CONFIDENTIAL

(U)   87.   That during the period 31 October - 23 November 1967 SCORPION conducted individual ship exercises and Weapons Systems Accuracy Tests (WSAT) while en route and in the Caribbean.

(U)   88.   That COMSUBRON 6 conducted an Administrative Inspection of SCORPION on 28-29 November 1967 and assigned an overall grade of "Excellent." (Ex 23)

(U)   89.   That SCORPION's Engineering Department was assigned a grade of "Outstanding" in this Administrative Inspection.

(U)   90.   That during the week of 4 December 1967 SCORPION engaged in type training exercises in the Virginia Capes area with COMSUBDIV 62 embarked.

(U) (FOUO)   91.   That SCORPION underwent a Nuclear Weapons Acceptance Inspection, conducted by COMSUBFLOT 6, on 19-20 December 1967 with the following results:

    a.   Technical operations were demonstrated in a competent professional manner.

    b.   Casualty drills were not demonstrated to the degree of established standards and SCORPION was assigned a grade of "Unsatisfactory."

COMSUBFLOT 6 conducted a reinspection on 5 January 1968, limited to a casualty drill and crew interviews. As a result SCORPION was assigned a grade of "Satisfactory" and certified for ASTOR. (Satisfactory and Unsatisfactory are the only grades considered.)

(C)(U) 92.   That in January 1968 SCORPION participated in an advanced submarine versus submarine exercise, and in the opinion of superiors, SCORPION performed least effectively of all the submarines involved, and this was attributable to Commander Slattery's lack of tactical experience in this phase of warfare.

(U)   93.   That the Inspector General, U. S. Atlantic Fleet, conducted a Damage Control Readiness Inspection of SCORPION in February 1968 and reported that the ship's ability to fight fires and combat damage was good.

(U)   94.   That witnesses, including the Administrative and Operational Commanders and former members of the crew of SCORPION, who spoke to the state of training and material readiness, expressed full confidence in the ship and its crew.

(U)   95.   That upon her deployment to the Mediterranean COMSUBLANT carried SCORPION in a C-1 or "fully combat ready" status in the four categories of training, personnel, supply, and material.

(U)   96.   That the Operations Officer, COMSUBFLOT 8 Staff, rode SCORPION from Rota, Spain, to Taranto, Italy, from 5-10 March. His observations led him to conclude that SCORPION was a well-trained, well-run submarine.

(W) 97. That Commander Submarine Florilla 8 conducted a nuclear safety inspection of SCORPION while she was in the Mediterranean and no major and only three minor discrepancies were found.

(U) 98. That SCORPION's performance in the Mediterranean was favorably noted by COMNAVSOUTH in NATO exercise Easy Gambler, and by COMSIXTHFLT in all the operations assigned.

(U) 99. That while on deployment in the Mediterranean Lieutenant Lamberth had relieved Lieutenant Burke as Weapons Officer; Lieutenant Flesch was understudying Lieutenant Commander Stephens in navigation but had not relieved him prior to departure from Rota, Spain.

(U) 100. That CINCUSNAVEUR certified SCORPION to be fully combat ready when she began her return trip from the Mediterranean to Norfolk in May.

(U) 101. That upon departure from Rota, Spain, on 17 May 1968, for return to Norfolk, Virginia, SCORPION carried 12 officers and 87 enlisted men. This was three officers and two enlisted men more than her allowance.

(U) 102. That as of 12 April 1968, seven of the 12 officers were qualified in submarines and 61 of the 87 enlisted men on board were qualified in submarines. Four of these enlisted men had qualified while deployed.

(U) 103. That both COMSUBRON 6 and COMSUBDIV 62 had observed and evaluated SCORPION and considered her well manned with respect to numbers, rates, job skills, and percentage of personnel qualified in submarines and they considered the Captain and the crew well trained and capable of safely operating the ship.

(U) 104. That four of the officers serving in SCORPION had submitted letters of resignation. They were:

Lieutenant William C. Harwi, USN,   Engineer Officer

Lieutenant George P. Farrin, USN,   Electrical Officer

Lieutenant John P. Burke, USN,   Assistant Engineer

Lieutenant Charles L. Lamberth, USN,   Weapons Officer

Each of the four officers cited purely personal reasons as the cause of his request.

(U) 105. That it was the view of the representative of the Bureau of Naval Personnel that the number of resignations submitted by SCORPION officers was greater than average, but that there is a trend toward more resignations throughout the submarine service.

It was also his expressed view that this trend is fostered by the direct

(U)   106.   That there is no evidence that any member of SCORPION's crew was suffer-ing from or had ever suffered from psychiatric illness.

(U) (FOUO)   107.   That psychiatric illness, per se, does not, under present rules, per-manently disqualify a person from submarine duty.

(U) (FOUO)   108.   That present rules permit an individual submarine medical officer, not necessarily trained in psychiatry, to authorize the requalification for submarine duty, of a man who has been disqualified previously for psychiatric reasons.

(U)   109.   That it was the normal practice on SCORPION to conduct emergency drills daily. Performance was usually observed by the Executive Officer and a critique of performance held after the drill. This practice was continued during her Mediterranean deployment.

(U)   110.   That in SCORPION a formal watch qualification program was conducted for supervisory watch stations with Commanding Officer and Executive Officer participation.

(U)   111.   That an extensive training program was conducted by SCORPION's crew while in the Norfolk Naval Shipyard, including emergency drills, and this training program was continued subsequent to the restricted availability.

(U)   112.   That the regular watches of Diving Officer and Chief of the Watch (Ballast Control Panel Operator) were combined and stood by one man, a Chief Petty Officer or Petty Officer First Class. The Auxiliaryman and/or IC Electrician of the Watch were normally in the Control Room area. A separate Diving Officer (commissioned officer) was used for Battle Stations, initial dives, and special or unusual circumstances.

(U)   113.   That the Officer of the Deck (OOD) was not permitted to leave the Con-trol Room/Attack Center area and normally stood his watch in close proximity to the ship control party.

(U)   114.   That at speeds above about 15 knots, it was standard practice to shift the stern planes to emergency, to position the stern planes near a zero angle, and to control depth within $\pm$ 10 feet using fairwater planes.

(U)   115.   That watertight doors were normally left open, including periods while handling and working on torpedoes and when coming to periscope depth.

(U)   116.   That operation of the oxygen system in SCORPION was the responsibility of the Auxiliaryman of the Watch for the forward station and the Engine Room Supervisor for the after station.

(U)   117.   That it was the normal procedure in SCORPION to bleed from the oxygen system during transits. Either the forward or after station was used, depending on the existing circumstances.

UNCLASSIFIED

(U) 118. That from evidence adduced, personnel in SCORPION were trained to consider, and it was normal practice to consider, recoverability studies in the selection of speed and depth during transits.

(C) 119. [That based on Predicted Safe Operating Limits and Emergency Recovery Capabilities for SSN585 Class submarines using recommended recovery measures SCORPION could recover from a stern plane jam on hard dive with initial speed (60) knots and initial depth [300] feet without exceeding [4(0)] feet. (Ex 67)

(U) 120. That during 1960, while operating at about 20 knots at about 200 feet, SCORPION on two occasions successfully recovered from stern plane failures to hard dive without exceeding design test depth by backing emergency without blowing main ballast tanks.

(U) 121. That SCORPION had a standard procedure for recovery from a stern plane jam on dive which prescribed backing full, fairwater planes on hard rise and blowing main ballast tanks.

(C) u 122. That in SSN585/588 Class submarines, the pitch angle of the ship would be in excess of [25° down angle in 10 seconds] if the stern planes failed to full dive at 20 knots and no recovery action was taken. However, if operating at a depth [of 300 feet or less,] recovery using recommended measures could still be effected before exceeding design test depth. (Ex 141)

(C) u 123. That based on evidence provided by COMSUBFLOT 8 the following excerpt from the concept of operations was promulgated by Commanding Officer, SCORPION, for use during NATO exercise DAWN PATROL: "9. Safety. The safety of the ship is paramount. Think in terms of a 'safety envelope' large enough to accommodate the ship (including conceivable ship control casualties) and adjusted to the precision with which we are able to navigate. No other ship, or the ground, are permitted within this envelope. As a general rule, the following procedures will be observed:

a. At speeds below 10 knots, always have at least 100 feet beneath the keel, and 60 feet above the sail (unless at periscope depth).

b. Do not go into water shallower than 35 fathoms submerged without my presence in the attack center.

c. At speeds 10 knots or greater, keep at least 15 feet per knot under the keel and at least 10 feet per knot plus 50 feet above the top of the sail (note that this permits operation at 20 knots at 300 feet in 100 fathoms)."

(Ex 164)

(X) 124. That based on Flooding Recovery Studies for SSN588 Class, from an initial depth of 300 feet SCORPION could recover from flooding casualties of the following severity:

At 5 knots initial speed: 7.5" ips hole

At 10 knots initial speed: 10.0" ips hole

At 20 knots initial speed: 16.0" ips hole

(Ex 66)

(U) 125. That the trash disposal unit (TDU) in SCORPION was normally operated at periscope depth and that the size of this circular opening to sea is about ten inches in diameter.

(U) ~~(FOUO)~~ 126. That the oxygen candle furnace had been located in the Torpedo Room of SCORPION but was moved to the vicinity of the CO_2 Scrubber Room prior to departure from Norfolk. There is no evidence that a continuous watch was assigned during operations on this unit. The furnace generates considerable heat.

(X)(U) 127. That the main pyrotechnic stowage locker on SCORPION was in the Torpedo Room and was floodable.

(X)(U) 128. That SCORPION Message 290837Z March 1968 reported having on board 70 submarine-type pyrotechnics and other miscellaneous small pyrotechnics and small arms ammunition normally carried by submarines.

(U) 129. That demolition charges were not issued to SCORPION prior to her departure from Norfolk for the Mediterranean and there is no evidence of any being on board at the time of her loss.

(U) 130. That SCORPION normally stored miscellaneous materials, such as canned foods, stores, bales of rags, extra lines, and clothing in the Torpedo Room when at sea for extended periods.

(U) 131. That it was standard procedure on SCORPION to collect dirty and oily rags in the Torpedo Room into special containers and to dispose of them through the TDU at the earliest practicable time.

(U) ~~(FOUO)~~ 132. That it is inherent in the operating systems and components of nuclear attack submarines that numerous fire hazards exist, such as lubricating oil, diesel oil, hydraulic oil, oxygen storage and generation (chlorate candles), combustible gases such as hydrogen, carbon monoxide, propane and methane. Since 1951 to the present time there have been recorded on JAG records a total of eight fires and explosions on SSNs.

(U) 133. That the 45-gallon alcohol storage tank in SCORPION, located on the starboard side of the Torpedo Room, was normally kept locked and access was controlled by the Weapons Officer and the Torpedo Room Watch.

(U)   134.   That the escape trunks were not used for the storage of any materials, stores, or equipage other than that required for escape purposes.

(U)   135.   That SCORPION stowed acetylene gas for cutting equipment in the Auxiliary Machinery Space and Pump Room.

(U)   136.   That when not installed in warheads, torpedo exploder mechanisms, arming devices, and boosters were normally stowed in special lockers in the Torpedo Room. Torpedo detonators were normally stowed in special containers in dispersed locations in the adjacent compartment.

(U)   137.   That all the torpedoes on SCORPION were stowed in the Torpedo Room (the forward compartment of the ship) either in the torpedo tubes or storage racks.

(S/RD)   138.   That the SCORPION had two MK 45 ASTOR torpedoes with associated MK 34 Mod 3 nuclear warheads on board at the time of her disappearance. Each of these warheads contains [( )] pounds of non-nuclear high explosive which could detonate if exposed to a fire of sufficient intensity, however, this would not cause a nuclear explosion. The crushing of this warhead by external water pressure would not cause an explosion of any kind.

(U)   139.   That a representative of the Nuclear Weapons Training Center, Atlantic, reported that the many safety features and stringent security pre- cautions associated with nuclear weapons makes it extremely unlikely that an accidental detonation could occur and that the radiation contamination hazard in the open ocean areas from a crushed or corroding nuclear warhead would be essentially negligible.

(U)   140.   That the SCORPION carried the following conventional torpedoes with associated warheads, boosters, detonators, and exploders:

                    7 MK 14-5
                    4 MK 37-0
                    10 MK 37-1

(U)   141.   That COMSUBLANT directs the use of check lists in torpedo preparation and authorizes the use of standard check lists contained in OPs covered by plastic document protectors and checked off with grease pencil. (Ex 177)

(U)   142   That the fuel for a MK 14 torpedo is ethyl alcohol which has a flash point of 48° to 52° F; the explosive limits are 3.5 to 19% by volume in air; and that the alcohol is not normally drained from torpedoes when preparing them for off-loading.

(C)   143.   That the MK 37 Mod 0 warhead associated with the MK 37 torpedoes contains about [( ) ( )] high explosive.

(U) (FOUO) 144. That inadvertent activation of the battery of a MK 37 torpedo has occurred on board submarines. COMSUBLANT Instruction 8510.35 CH-1 of 25 October 1966 advises ships of the danger of such inadvertent activation and emphasizes the importance of following test procedures contained in check-off sheets in NAVWEPS ODs and OPs.

(C) 145. That prior to jettisoning a MK 37 Mod 0 or Mod 1 tactical torpedo the prescribed action includes removing or sterilizing the exploder. This requires removal of the torpedo from the torpedo tube. The OPs contain the following: "WARNING. Do not allow the fin velocity switch to operate during the time the torpedo is withdrawn from the tube. The arming cycle of the exploder starts as soon as the fin switch is operated."

(C) 146. That a Torpedo Firing Report submitted by SCORPION for a MK 37 Mod 1 exercise torpedo fired on 5 December 1967 contains the following comments: "Unit was a hot run in the tube. Approximately 4 minutes prior to starting, the torpedo had been warmed up. However, it would not accept depth input. In addition, an intermittent 'set' light for the anti-capture setting was being received. Suspecting a short in the firing/transmission circuit, power to the tube was secured. Another torpedo tube was selected and a MK37-1 was fired without abnormality."

"Approximately 2 1/2 minutes after the successful firing, the first unit started in the tube. The torpedo tube did not fire when the unit started, indicating a stray voltage in the torpedo or A Cable. Due to personnel error, the torpedo was allowed to swim out of the tube. It was not recovered. Inspection of the A Cable indicated a clean cut with no evidence of any other marks, cuts or faults." (Ex 185)

(C)(U) 147. That in November 1967, through personnel error, one exercise torpedo MK 45 Mod 1 was inadvertently impulsed out of the torpedo tube rather than being allowed to swim out. (Ex 173)

(FOUO) 148. That SCORPION's procedure for inadvertent activation of a tactical MK 37
(C) torpedo in a torpedo tube was to flood the tube to keep the torpedo cool, turn the ship to cause the /B/ to shut down the propulsion motor of the torpedo, drain the tube, open the tube inner door, install the propeller lock, and jettison the torpedo.

(C) 149. That the anti-circular run circuit of a MK 37 torpedo is designed to stop the torpedo if it turns more than 170° from the launch tube heading before the torpedo enables.

(C) 150. That the anti-circular run feature of a MK 37 torpedo is disabled when the torpedo has enabled.

(C) 151. That, while the minimum enabling distance that can be set in a MK 37 torpedo is 300 yards, which equates to about 21 seconds of torpedo run time in high speed, the torpedo settings will generally be unknown when the torpedo is accidentally activated and stratum protection might be unavailable to the firing vessel.

SECRET UNCLASSIFIED

(C)(u) 152. That enabling and arming of a MK 37 torpedo is designed to commence when the [fin velocity switch actuates upon launch] of the weapon.

(U) 153. That NAVWEPS OPs covering torpedo MK 14 Mod 5 and exploder mechanism MK 6 Mod 13 specify installation and removal of exploder mechanism and booster with the exploder cavity of the torpedo facing upward.

(C)(u) 154. That SCORPION's leading torpedoman for five years, detached 22 December 1967, testified that the procedure normally followed for arming and disarming MK 14 Mod 5 torpedo warheads was to rotate the torpedo so that the axis of the exploder cavity was canted at a slight angle from the vertical. Working from below the warhead, as the exploder was being lowered, a man would insert his hand into the exploder cavity and catch the booster.

(C)(u) 155. That the MK 19 exploder mechanism used in the MK 37 torpedo is designed to delay mechanically arming the exploder until about [15 seconds] after the torpedo exits the launching tube and attains a [speed of about 13 knots.] It is also designed to delay energizing the firing circuit until the torpedo [enables.]

(C)(u) 156. That the MK 16 Mod 6 warhead associated with the MK 14-5 torpedo contains about [643 pounds of HBX-3] high explosive.

(C)(u) 157. That it had been over one year since SCORPION had conducted an operation which required tactical torpedoes to be fully ready; since her last operation all of her torpedo "gang" had been replaced and her Weapons Officer had been relieved.

(U) 158. That there were eight torpedoman on board SCORPION, one of whom was the Chief of the Boat. This was three torpedoman more than their allowance, and the rates were in excess of allowance. (Ex 25)

(U) 159. That in the opinion of the Squadrons Weapons Officer and the former leading torpedoman they were an experienced "gang" comparable to and probably above the average torpedo "gang" in their squadron.

(U) 160. That during the period between refresher training in October-December 1967 SCORPION fired 29 exercise torpedoes two of which were lost.

(C)(u) 161. That the Operation Order under which SCORPION operated subsequent to departure from the Mediterranean about 170001Z does not definitely specify [whether or not torpedoes should be in a fully ready condition.]

(U) 162. That SCORPION was scheduled to off-load all torpedoes upon return to Norfolk incident to a drydocking at the Norfolk Naval Shipyard.

(C)(u) 163. That the route prescribed by the operational commander for SCORPION's transit from south of the Azores to Norfolk passed about eight miles from the charted 13-fathom sounding in the vicinity of Cruiser Sea

(U) 164. That the pertinent bottom contour charts covering SCORPION's directed track from her last reported position to CONUS were: BC 306, BC 406, BC 506, BC 507, BC 607, BC 707, BC 807 - all issued prior to 1965.

(C)(U) 165. That COMSUBLANT Instruction 03430.5 of 9 April 1963 directed that these bottom contour charts be maintained on board SSNs and during the Administrative Inspection in November 1967 a spot check of SCORPION's bottom contour charts indicated that the proper charts were on board.

(U) 166. That during an Administrative Inspection of the SCORPION's Navigation Department in November 1967 a spot check of approximately 25 charts indicated that SCORPION had the latest editions and that these charts were correct and up to date.

(C)(U) 167. That in the vicinity of SCORPION's last reported position and westward along her prescribed track to 40°W, the bottom contour charts presently in use indicate that the charts were constructed over 90% of the area from sounding line spacing of greater than 25 miles and in some areas greater than 50 miles. In this area during the search for SCORPION, sea mounts were discovered in some areas where none were indicated on the bottom contour charts; and, conversely, careful survey was unable to locate certain sea mounts that were indicated on the charts.

(U) 168. That the bottom contour charts currently in general use for submerged navigation were constructed from information obtained over a period of many years from sources of questionable accuracy, both in navigation and soundings. These bottom contour charts were the only bottom contour charts available to SCORPION to be used as an aid of navigation in determining ship's position.

(C)(U) 169. That in 1968 the USS THEODORE ROOSEVELT (SSBN600), while transiting through the Londonderry Operating Areas at 200 feet keel depth, was extensively damaged when she collided with the sea bottom which reached to within 138 feet of the surface.

(C)(U)170. That ROOSEVELT was using NAVOCEANO Confidential Chart HO 17,326-1-OA issued in June 1964 which indicated a charted depth of 50 to 60 fathoms at the point of bottoming.

(U) 171. That during the transit to the Mediterranean in the vicinity of the Azores when the SCORPION's position was in doubt, the Commanding Officer, the Executive Officer, and the Navigator had all shown concern about the presence of sea mounts and inaccuracies of the bottom contour charts. On this occasion the ship slowed, decreased depth, and obtained continuous soundings.

(U) 172. That the AN/UQN-1D fathometer on SCORPION was located in close proximity to the Chief of the Watch's station rather than the navigation work area. It was usual procedure for the Chief of the Watch to obtain and have recorded a sounding at least once every 30 minutes when underway. The Navigator made a practice of taking continuous soundings whenever a periodic sounding did not agree with the charted depth.

(U) 173. That the Submarine Safety Center did, in February 1966, express concern to the CNO about the increased hazard of submerged collision with uncharted pinnacles and sea mounts in the light of increased depth and speed capabilities of modern submarines.

(U) 174. That the Submarine Safety Center did, in February 1966, recommend survey, resurvey, and issuance of new charts for all areas in which submarines may operate.

(U) 175. That USS GATO (SSN 615) reported the bottom contour charts to the west of longitude 30°W along SCORPION's directed track were not of sufficient accuracy to permit reliable bottom contour navigation.

(U) 176. That no pinnacles or unusual topographical formations were detected on top of Cruiser Sea Mount or Hyeres Bank nor in the immediate vicinity which would constitute a hazard to submerged operations by SCORPION at her restricted depth.

(U) 177. That neither the 26 nor 13 fathom charted pinnacles adjacent to Cruiser Sea Mount were located by the search force and no soundings of less than 128 fathoms were reported in the general area.

(U) 178. That in the vicinity of SCORPION's last reported position, daytime accuracies of 3 to 5 miles could be expected using LORAN A Chain DELTA, however, during night time this accuracy could be considerably reduced because of skywave and other electronic interference. LORAN A Chain DELTA, operated by the Portuguese under NATO agreement, is provided with an alarm system to alert operating personnel to any important irregularity in the operation of the stations. There were no important irregularities reported by any station in LORAN A Chain DELTA during the period 202000Z through 272400Z May.

(U) 179. That in the area of SCORPION's last reported position and westward along her entire prescribed track, the LORAN coverage from all chains was

CONFIDENTIAL

(U)   180.   That the pertinent LORAN A charts covering SCORPION's directed track on return to CONUS were: VL30-22, VL30-23, VL30-24 - all issued in 1966 or earlier.

(N)(u) 181.   That COMSUBLANT Instruction 03530.5 of 9 April 1963, which specified charts to be maintained by various classes of submarines, did not direct that these LORAN A charts be maintained on board all SSNs, however, this instruction did not preclude their use.

(N)(u) 182.   That CINCLANTFLT letter serial 0534/J25 of 11 April 1968 revised the chart requirements for SSNs and does require these LORAN A charts be maintained on board, but this letter was not mailed until 8 May 1968 after SCORPION had left Naples, Italy, on operations which were planned to terminate in CONUS. On 4 March 1968 while in Rota, Spain, SCORPION obtained from CANOPUS a number of charts including VL30-23 and VL30-25 LORAN A charts and could have obtained VL30-24 if she requested it.

(U)   183.   That during the transit to the Mediterranean SCORPION did experience difficulties with LORAN navigation in the eastern Atlantic.

(U)   184.   That SCORPION's LORAN C was calibrated on CANOPUS, checked satisfactorily, and returned to SCORPION prior to entering the Mediterranean.

(U)   185.   That normally the Chief Quartermaster or First Class Quartermaster took LORAN fixes, however, the other quartermasters also took LORAN fixes.

(U)   186.   That the leading quartermaster on board SCORPION was Senior Chief Petty Officer MAZZUCHI who has been attached to and serving on board for over six years. A previous navigator reported that Senior Chief Petty Officer MAZZUCHI was an extremely talented quartermaster and operated the navigation equipment of the ship very competently.

(U)   187.   That the Navigation Department enlisted personnel were of the authorized rate and ratings.

(U)   188.   That outside observers noticed that SCORPION's navigation personnel habitually used all of their available navigation systems, including celestial observations, and checked the systems against each other.

(U)   189.   That Commander Submarine Division 62, in his personal letter 1-67 of 3 November 1967, directed Commanding Officers' attention to good navigational practices and during underway visits had observed SCORPION's navigational personnel to be using such practices. (Ex 24)

(U)   190.   That since June 1967, Lieutenant Commander Daniel P. STEPHENS, USN, had been the ship's Navigator and was not scheduled to be relieved until return to CONUS. The Commanding Officer considered him to be competent and cautious and commended him on at least three occasions for his performance. He normally placed primary reliance on LORAN A for navigation, but did use other systems available to him, including

(U)   192. That for any given operational situation, the Commanding Officer did specify CAUTION and DANGER soundings which required immediate action to be taken by the OOD in order to further enhance the safe navigation of the ship.

(S)(U) 193. That SCORPION had the following navigation equipment installed:

    a. Master Gyro Compass, MK 19 Mod 3A.
    b. Auxiliary Gyro Compass, MK23 Mod 0.
    c. Magnesyn Compass with emergency battery power supply.
    d. Dead Reckoning Analyzer Indicator MK 5 Mod 3.
    e. Dead Reckoning Tracer, MK 7 Mod 2.
    f. MK 19 Plotter.
    g. UPN-12 LORAN A Receiver.
    h. WPN-4 LORAN C Receiver.
    i. Type III 8B Periscope Sextant.
    j. AN/BQN-4A Fathometer.
    k. AN/UQN-1D Fathometer.

(U)   194. That SCORPION did not normally use active sonar, other than the fathometer, for navigational safety during submerged transit.

(U)   195. That there was an outstanding Casualty Report (CASREP) on the MK 19 Plotter because of a lack of repair parts, however, the lack of these parts would not prevent the Plotter from functioning as a dead reckoning position keeper.

(U)   196. That an outstanding work request reported the Type III 8B Periscope Sextant was out of alignment.

(U)   197. That while an outstanding work request reported the WPN-4 LORAN C Receiver inoperable with the velocity motor energized, it could still be used manually for position determination.

(U)   198. That COMSUBLANT promulgates promptly by message to the Submarine Force, Atlantic, information concerning newly discovered hazards to submerged navigation.

(U)   199. That COMSUBLANT sent information concerning chart inaccuracies, compiled from classified sources, to the U.S. Naval Oceanographic Office (NAVOCEANO) to assist in updating charts.

(U)   200. That information concerning inaccuracies noted on bottom contour charts is disseminated by NAVOCEANO by Navy Notices to Mariners which require about three weeks in preparation, printing, and mailing.

(S)(U) 201. That there were no Notices to Mariners issued since 1964 which indicated a hazard to SCORPION in the vicinity of her last reported position and westward along her prescribed track to the vicinity of the acoustic event about 221844Z May.

UNCLASSIFIED

(U) (FOUO) 203. That NAVOCEANO considers their present funding and staffing to be essentially adequate, but that more personnel would be required if the volume of information to be processed were increased.

(C) (U) 204. That recently NAVOCEANO has proposed a system of Notices to Submerged Mariners to correct NAVOCEANO products primarily used by Fleet Ballistic Missile (FBM) submarines.

(U) 205. That COMSUBLANT and COMSUBPAC are in general agreement that the navigation product improvement in support of the FBM weapon system should be expanded to include support to all submarines, with priority being given to areas of highest submarine operating density.

(U) 206. That since 1962, ocean charting programs have been under the cognizance of the Defense Intelligence Agency (DIA) which requires that requests for products or special surveys be submitted via Unified and Specified Commands.

(S) 207. That in November 1965, COMSUBLANT submitted via CINCLANT/CINCLANTFLT to DIA an urgent request for updating present bottom contour charts using all available data and for development of new bottom contour charts. The content of the charts were requested to be such that contour intervals and topographical characteristics would permit navigational accuracy to within two nautical miles and cover all ocean areas in which U.S. submarines operate.

In their endorsement dated 6 January 1966, DIA accepted as a priority and valid operational requirement the "... (1)

contour charts." . DIA further stated that "... adequate provision should be included in the Consolidated Intelligence Program now in preparation to assure the continued timely update of bottom contour and nonsubmarine contacts charts . ." in support of oceanographic requirements. (Ex 124)

(C) (U) 208. That the U.S. Navy has under evaluation a new type of bottom contour chart named BATHYMETRIC NAVIGATION CHART (BNC) which is considered by NAVOCEANO to be a quantum improvement over the bottom contour charts presently in general use for submerged navigation in open ocean areas.

(C) (U) 209. That at present, according to information from NAVOCEANO, there is no long range plan authorized to fully exploit the potential of the bottom survey system which produces BNC charts, except in support of the FBM weapons system or special projects such as Project Caesar.

(C) (U) 210. That there is no program presently planned to systematically survey the oceans for sea mounts.

(C) (U) 211. That with the recent advent of the satellite navigation system and advanced array bottom survey equipment a capability now exists to

(C)   212.   That NAVOCEANO considers that the navigation and depth recording systems used to obtain the information for [BNC charts] are of such accuracy and detail that in the area surveyed it is very unlikely that a sea mount would remain undetected.

(C) (U)   213.   That the United States has only four ships [(DUTTON, BOWDITCH, MICHAELSON, and COMPASS ISLAND)] equipped to conduct these surveys, with only three of these ships routinely engaged in oceanographic work. At present only a very limited area of the ocean has been surveyed using this system.

(U) (FOUO)   214.   That a detailed and accurate survey using this new system in the vicinity of SCORPION's last reported position, including the Cruiser Sea Mount and Hyeres Bank areas, detected no sounding of less than 128 fathoms.

(C)(U)   215.   That in March 1968, the CNO requested the Chief of Naval Material to conduct a Cost and Feasibility Study leading to installation of the Navigational Satellite System in all SSNs, post-WWII SSs, and Guppy III SSs in the shortest possible time.

(U)   216.   That since the loss of THRESHER in 1963, extensive measures have been taken to reduce operational casualties to submarines.

(U) (FOUO)   217.   That since 1963, the three main casualties to SSN585/588 Class submarines as identified by COMSUBLANT were: a fire in USS SHARK, a flooding casualty in USS SCULPIN, and a grounding of USS SCAMP.

(U)(C)   218.   That since 1963 there have been three explosion casualties in submarines of the Atlantic Fleet, all in electrolytic oxygen generator plants in SSBNs. (Ex 183)

(U)   219.   That electrolytic oxygen generators were not installed in SCORPION.

(C)   220.   That the only reported problem associated with the nuclear power plant was an inoperative [⊂ ⊬ (/)   ⊐] valve shut position indicator.

(C)   221.   That following SCRAM of the reactor plant the residual heat is sufficient to drive the main turbines for about eight minutes at a speed corresponding to a propeller shaft speed of about [⊂ ⊬ (/)   ⊐]. Higher speeds are possible for correspondingly shorter periods.

(U)   222.   That the Associate Director for Submarines, Division of Naval Reactors, Atomic Energy Commission stated that the reactors used in all U. S. submarines are designed to minimize potential hazards to the environment even under most severe casualty conditions, such as sinking of the ship. Some of these design features are:

1.   The reactor core is so designed that it is physically impossible for it to explode like a bomb.

2.   The reactor's fuel elements are made of materials that are extremely corrosion resistant, even in sea water.

3. Where the reactor is completely submerged in sea water, the fuel elements will remain intact for an indefinite period of time and the radioactive material contained in these fuel elements would not be released.

4. Radioactive material could be released from this type of reactor only if the fuel elements were actually to melt and, in addition, the high-strength, all-welded reactor boundary were to rupture.

5. The reactor's many protective devices and self-regulating features are designed to prevent automatically any melting of the fuel elements.

6. Flooding of the reactor with sea water furnishes additional cooling for the fuel elements and so provides added protection against the release of radioactive material.

7. If the ship were sunk, it is expected that the reactor core could remain submerged in sea water for decades without release of fission products, since the protective cladding on the fuel elements corrodes only a few millionths of an inch per year.

8. The maximum rate of release and dispersal of the radioactivity in the ocean, even if the protective cladding on the fuel were destroyed, would be so low as to be harmless.

He further stated that it is highly unlikely that the reactor pressure vessel would be ruptured because it is expected that pressure inside and outside the reactor pressure vessel would be equalized by sea water entering the reactor plant, probably through either rupture of small piping or seal welds.

(C)(u) 223. That the Submarine Safety (SUBSAFE) work performed (or not undertaken for the reasons indicated) by Charleston Naval Shipyard during SCORPION's RO in 1963-1964, as specified by the Naval Ships Systems Command (NAVSHIPS) ltr ser 525-0267 of 27 August 1963 and as authorized by DEPCOMSUBLANT msg 272000Z Aug 63, cost $1,277,140 of the total overhaul cost of $3,729,760 and is summarized as follows:

1.a. For [sea water systems] all pipe joints between hull and back-up valves were ultrasonically tested (UT) to assure 60% bond or were replaced by welded joints. (Note: current SUBSAFE specifications require minimum 60% bond on all silbrazed joints 1/2" ips or larger that are UTed.)

1.b. For sea water systems inboard of the back-up valve, all brazed pipe joints 4 inches and larger were UT inspected to assure 60% bond and all pipe joints worked on between 1/2 inch and 4 inches were certified 60% bond.

3. For the oxygen system, all joints were welded.

4.a. For hydraulic systems, stern diving and steering, all joints were certified 60% bond or welded in the pressure piping between the steering and stern diving rams and the hydraulic pump discharge plus the suction piping between the pumps and supply tank.

4.b. A remote emergency sea water valve closing system was not authorized and was not installed.

5. All flexible connections in critical piping systems were inspected and replaced in accordance with NAVSHIP's letter ser 648L/2420 of 22 December 1961. End fittings were inspected and replaced, as necessary, with the then existing type and fittings.

6. All new cast fittings, 4 inches and larger, were inspected radiographically but complete replacement of all hull and back-up valves was not authorized.

7. Aluminum bronze inspections were completed on all hull and back-up valve bonnets in systems subject to sea pressure, on torpedo muzzle and breech doors, and on other accessible components.

8. All hull and back-up valve bolts and studs were inspected visually and by acid spot test and verified as non-ferrous or replaced by monel fasteners.

9. Copper nickel tubing inspection was not a required test at time of SCORPION overhaul.

10. An interim EMBT blow system was designed and installed by Charleston Naval Shipyard but was evaluated as unsuitable for service and made inoperable at the direction of NAVSHIPS.

11. Access to vital equipment was not a required test for SCORPION overhaul.

12. Stern plane reliability items were not authorized for accomplishment.

SCORPION did have a positive means for control of the stern diving power transfer valve from the control station.

The SSN585 Class stern diving hydraulic system is the standard for reliability when making a design review for other class submarines.

The 150% hydrostatic test of the stern diving hydraulic system was performed.

13. All tapered thread fittings outboard of back-up valves were replaced by welded fittings.

UNCLASSIFIED

CONFIDENTIAL

15. The work accomplished on the oxygen system, the stern diving and steering hydraulic systems and the tapered thread fittings exceeded the current SUBSAFE specifications. (Exs 57, 57a)

(U) 224. That the evaluation of the Charleston overhaul by SCORPION's Commanding Officer was that the vast proportion of work was satisfactorily performed and deficiencies cited were subsequently corrected by Forces Afloat. (Ex 61)

(U) 225. That a Submarine Safety Program was established by NAVSHIPS as a result of the THRESHER loss; that the program provides the criteria for certification of submarines for unrestricted operation to designed test depth and the continuing development of safety improvement items which will further enhance operating safety; and that the certification criteria was promulgated by BUSHIPS ltr ser 525-0462 of 20 December 1963. (Ex 62)

(U) 226. That the SUBSAFE certification criteria is directed to four principal areas:

   1. Establishing piping system and hull boundary integrity.

   2. Improving emergency recoverability.

   3. Increasing stern plane reliability, and

   4. Providing a continuing record for proof of certification.

(U) 227. That NAVSHIPS and the Submarine Force Commanders have established policy and procedures for the purchase of SUBSAFE materials and for maintaining the continuity of SUBSAFE certification during the operating cycle. (Exs 49,51)

(C)(U) 228. That the accomplishment of SUBSAFE certification has not been deferred due to the lack of funds, but has been deferred on some submarines because of:

   a. The lack of industrial overhaul capacity, naval and private,

   b. The delayed deliveries of long lead time materials,

   c. The lack of commercial sources for special certified materials,

   d. The operational needs of the fleet for more ship on-line time.

   (Ex 63)

(C)(U) 229. That SUBSAFE work was deferred on SCORPION during the RAV at Norfolk in 1967 on the basis of:

c. Emergency recovery capability of installed systems,

d. Manday capacity available at Norfolk Naval Shipyard, and

e. Unavailability of long lead time material items.

(C) 230. That one of the SUBSAFE certification requirements is an EMBT blow system having the capacity and capability to recover from a single, [b (1)] diameter hole of unrestricted opening under the following conditions:

1. Ship at test depth, neutral buoyancy and zero trim at time of casualty,

2. Ship speed of 5 knots immediately before casualty,

3. Immediate loss of propulsion after casualty,

4. Flooding in the engine room,

5. Recovery action initiated within [b (1)] seconds,

6. Air bank pressure in all banks at [b (1)] psi,

7. Control surfaces on zero and remain on zero during recovery evolution,

8. Ballast tank blow initiated b(1) seconds after casualty occurs,

9. Flooding secured b(1) seconds after casualty occurs,

10. No part of the ship exceeds collapse depth during recovery evolutions, and

11. Ship considered surfaced when any part of pressure hull broaches the surface.

(C) 231. That the ballast blow systems, normal and emergency, provide the following hole size flooding recoverability:

Depth/Blow System:	585/588 Class		593 Class		
	Normal MBT	EMBT	Normal MBT	Interim EMBT	Full EMBT
	b (1)				
	b (1)				

(U) 232. That the normal main ballast tank blow system, as originally designed

(U) 233. That SCORPION had demonstrated her normal main ballast tank blow system would not freeze up by a full air tank blow down.

(U) 234. That SCORPION had not reported any operational problems with the normal main ballast tank blow system and that there were no repair work request items pending on the normal main ballast tank blow system.

(C) 235. That the best estimated minimum collapse depth for principal pressure hull compartments, tanks, trunks, and bulkheads are as follows:

ITEM		BEST EST. OF MINIMUM COLLAPSE DEPTH (IN FT.)
PRESSURE HULL -	Fwd Closure Bkhd	
	Torpedo Room	
	Control Room	
	Reactor Comp.	
	Aux Mach Space	
	Engine Room	
	Aft Closure Bkhd	
INTERNAL BKHDS-	Fwd Holding, Fr.	
	Fwd Reactor Compt, Fr	
	Aft Reactor Compt, Fr.	
	Aft Holding, Fr	
TRUNKS -	Fwd Escape	
	Bridge Access	
	After Escape	
HARD TANKS -	WRT	
	Fwd Trim	
	Sanitary #1 and #2	
	Negative Tank	
	Auxiliary #1 & #2	
	Sanitary #3	
	Aft Trim	(Ex 146)

(U) 236. That the pressure hull of SCORPION was constructed of HY-80 steel.

(U) 237. That exhaustive tests have established that HY-80 is a tough material; it is not notch sensitive even in cold water and under stress loading; and, cracks do not propagate rapidly or cause catastrophic failures. (Ex 65)

(C) 238. That tests, and the interpretation thereof by competent experts, reveal that the stress induced into the pressure hull structure by high frequency vibrations of attachments and appendages is extremely low and does not represent a structural fatigue problem; and, that HY-80 castings have fatigue characteristics equal to or better than comparable weldments. (Exs 144, 145)

(U) 239. That the low cycle fatigue studies have been evaluated by NAVSHIPS for the SSN585/588 Classes, including SCORPION, and that the areas of highest stress are monitored by the HY-80 Hull Surveillance Program.

(C) 240. That the Hull Surveillance Program, established by NAVSHIPS in 1960, to monitor and assure structural soundness of HY-80 submarine hulls, has been applicable to SCORPION since her completion; and that following the last hull surveillance inspection at Norfolk Naval Shipyard during the 1967 RAV, NAVSHIPS rated SCORPION's hull "good" for operations to the restricted depth of $h(l)$ feet. (Ex 64)

(U) 241. That on 1 July 1966, NAVSHIPS revised and promulgated a change to the Standard Naval Shipyard Regulations Manual. This revision, applicable to all Naval Shipyards, established a Quality and Reliability Assurance Department (QRAD) reporting directly to the Shipyard Commander. The review of Norfolk Naval Shipyard's Quality and Reliability Assurance Department, made for the Court, found this department organized in accordance with the regulation requirements and verified the accuracy and correctness of the evidence presented of work accomplished during SCORPION's 1967 RAV on her hull and back-up valves, and hydraulic transfer line. (Ex 186)

(U) 242. That SCORPION deployed to the Mediterranean with a minor hull crack indication found during hull surveillance inspection by ORION. This was evaluated by COMSUBLANT as satisfactory for continued operations and WR 2609 of 4 January was submitted to assure repair of this indication at the next RAV.

(S) 243. That a contact explosion of [$h(l)$] of TNT or equivalent, in water, will cause a lethal rupture in the HY-80 hull of SCORPION; and, that a non-contact explosion, in water, requires a shock factor of [   ] or greater for lethal damage to her hull.

(S) 244. That there is no technical information, supported by experimental data, to accurately predict the effect of an explosion inside a submarine pressure hull on the structures or personnel. It is estimated by the Naval Ship Research and Development Center (NSRDC) that an internal explosion of more than [$h(l)$] located near the center of the torpedo room would be required to rupture the pressure hull and that a charge of about [$h(l)$] would be fatal to all personnel within a 15 foot radius. (Ex 147, 171)

(U) 245. That SCORPION's principal hydraulic power plants were located in the after end of the Engine Room, port and starboard, in close proximity to each other.

(U) 246. That the design of SCORPION's principal hydraulic systems provides multiple and separable power supplies and multiple hydraulic power plant arrangements such that a single electric power casualty or hydraulic power plant failure will not cause the total loss of

(U)   247.   That hydraulic cleanliness standards were formally promulgated by
               NAVSHIPS in 1965 for the maintenance of submarine hydraulic systems.
               (Ex 127)

(U)   248.   That SCORPION reported no continuing past history of salt water
               contamination or other specific hydraulic problems.   (Ex 160, 180)

(U)   249.   That analysis of SCORPION hydraulic oil samples in January 1968 met
               the requirements for operational cleanliness except for the external
               hydraulic system and the particulate count above the 250 micron size
               in all systems.

(U)   250.   That a hydraulic oil sample analysis report by ORION, dated 5 February,
               states, "too much salt water to analyze" on one sample from the vital
               return from the Torpedo Room.

(U)   251.   That on 14 February a flush of SCORPION's hydraulic systems was
               completed using particulate filter equipment; and that there is no
               record of oil sample analysis after the flush was completed.

(U)   252.   That SCORPION had used large quantities of hydraulic oil enroute to
               the Mediterranean due to leakage in the fairwater planes and/or the
               periscope hydraulic systems; that she drew lubricating oil and
               hydraulic oil from CANOPUS on arrival at Rota.   (Ex 156)

(U)   253.   That SCORPION experienced vibration of the stern area during the
               operating period from 9 to 19 November 1967 which was attributed to
               air in the hydraulic system; that an unidentified "bump or thump"
               noise occurred in the stern area during the October 1967 sea trials
               following the RAV at Norfolk; and that inspections were made by
               ORION divers following each incident without finding the cause.

(U)   254.   That SCORPION experienced rudder failure to full left rudder on
               19 February 1968, enroute to the Mediterranean.

(U)   255.   That SCORPION had experienced stern plane failures to full dive but
               that plane control in the emergency mode was achieved in each instance
               cited since modification of the stern plane control system in 1961.

(U)   256.   That the stern plane hydraulic system in normal mode of operation is
               provided with means to automatically or manually transfer control
               to the emergency mode resulting from loss of normal hydraulic power
               and for electrical faults such as loss of power, magnetic amplifier
               failure, servo control valve shorts and grounds.   (Ex 151)

(U)   257.   That control of the stern planes in the emergency mode by-passes all
               electrical control circuits such that loss of plane control can
               occur only by total loss of vital hydraulic power or a mechanical
               failure between the diving power ram and the stern planes.

(C)(U) 258. That, for the condition of total loss of hydraulic power between the power transfer valve and the power ram or of the mechanical linkage between the power ram and the stern planes, i.e., "free planes", test data is not available to predict the position and reactions of the stern planes and the effect on the submarine.

(C)(U) 259. That power transfer valves, solenoid control valves and other hydraulic control components, manufactured of 2000 series (2014-T6) aluminum alloys, have failed due to stress corrosion cracking (induced by salt water contamination of hydraulic oil) and fatigue cracking; that the incidence of cracking has been very low in the valves from one manufacturer; that the failures experienced to date have not resulted in total loss of planes or rudder control.

(C)(U) 260. That SCORPION's power transfer valves for diving and steering control systems were manufactured of 2014-T6 aluminum alloy by the manufacturer whose valves have had the lowest incidence of cracking; and that SCORPION's solenoid control valves and other control components were manufactured of 6061-T6 aluminum alloy.

(U) 261. That NAVSHIPS has established a program to replace the 2000 series aluminum alloy hydraulic control valves with titanium components.

(C)(U) 262. That NAVSHIPS has a program for continued improvement of stern diving plane reliability which includes, but is not limited to, the following:

a. Independent steering and diving system power plants,

b. Stored energy accumulator for stern planes,

c. Vernier control of stern planes,

d. Dual stern plane rams,

e. Power transfer valves integral with stern plane rams,

f. Physically separated steering and diving hydraulic power plants,

g. Stern plane physical stop for limiting angles.

That design feasibility studies have been completed on the above items; that portions of the program are in the hardware testing stage; that SHIPALTS are being prepared for some items; and that some are being incorporated into current new construction projects. (Ex 117)

(U) 263. That COMSUBLANT has expressed a need for achieving maximum stern plane system reliability commensurate with military requirements as a matter of utmost urgency. (Ex 174)

(U) (FOUO) 264. That SCORPION's 3000 psi oxygen system

c. was equipped with a remote closure feature for the oxygen bank stop valves,

d. was an all welded system,

e. was operated under a ship doctrine requiring that the banks not be bled below a pressure of about 500 psi,

f. piping was located well clear of torpedo room work areas,

g. had diffusers installed to mix the oxygen with surrounding air,

h. had a diffuser in the torpedo room located aft and overhead next to a ventilation line exhaust,

i. had been discharged and recharged at least once since October 1967.

(U)   265. That there were no known problems with the oxygen system and no repair work was requested or accomplished on the oxygen system during the RAV at Norfolk Naval Shipyard or by ORION during subsequent upkeep periods.

(U) 266. That oxygen

a. in concentrations of over 26 to 30% or by direct stream impingement can cause spontaneous ignition of combustible materials.

b. by itself, will not burn or explode.

c. explosions and fires have occurred on

1. SARGO – caused by failure of charging line from oxygen charging truck.

2. SHARK – caused by hydraulic ignition of oil contaminants at low pressure during charging operations.

(U)   267. That Freon –12

a. was the refrigerant in SCORPION's air conditioning and refrigeration systems,

b. tests on animals, conducted in a 20% Freon atmosphere, showed no noticeable ill effects,

c. is an innocuous gas which will not cause ill effects to humans provided that the partial pressure of oxygen is maintained,

d. if totally released to the sealed boat atmosphere from one of SCORPION's air conditioning plants, would have resulted in a

(U)   268.   That SCORPION, during her Mediterranean deployment,

    a.   drew about 500 pounds of Freon,

    b.   operated for extensive periods of time in a sealed boat condition with no ill effects reported,

    c.   had Freon leakage which was mentioned by the Commanding Officer in his letters to his Division Commander as a continuing problem but not a hazard,

    d.   had Freon leakage associated with gage lines and not major components,

    e.   had submitted three work requests for repairs to the 1/8 inch gage lines of her air conditioning and refrigeration plants,

    f.   had modified her Atmosphere Control Bill to include more stringent control of Freon.

(U)   269.   That SCORPION's main storage battery was a Gould type TLX-53A, with over one year guaranteed service life remaining, that the battery produced 106% capacity when tested in January 1968, and that hydrogen gas generation on this battery had not been reported as a problem.

(U)   270.   That hydrogen gas generated by main storage batteries on submarines is monitored and controlled by special equipment and systems, such as hydrogen detectors, battery ventilation air flow meters, atmosphere analysers and $CO-H_2$ burners.

(C)(U) 271.   That NAVSHIPS has classified the probability of explosions from various sources, components and systems and estimated the effects therefrom; and that the following are from the NAVSHIPS summary:

Source	Likelihood	Effects Estimated
(a) Hydrogen gas from storage battery	Very low	Some personnel casualties but hull damage not probable.
(b) Hydraulic lines	Very low	Local effects, very low.
(c) High pressure air	Minimal	Extensive local equipment and personnel damage but any hull damage doubtful.
(d) Lube oil and fuel oil systems	Unlikely	Minor.
(e) Miscellaneous gases such as CO, O_2 bleed	Remote	Low magnitude, unless associated with a major

(g) Ammunition, small arms	Highly unlikely	Local damage and personnel hazard but no danger of ship loss if allowance all detonated simultaneously.
(h) Pyrotechnics	Highly unlikely	Slight to moderate damage; no loss of ship if all pyrotechnics exploded simultaneously

(Ex 167)

(U) ~~(FOUO)~~ 272. That SCORPION's Ship Alteration and Improvement (A&I) status was:

    a. 106 ShipAlts reported complete

         7 ShipAlts reported partially completed

      166 ShipAlts outstanding

    b.   74 A&I items reported complete

       69 A&I items outstanding   (Ex 10)

(U) 273. That COMSUBLANT stated that the nonaccomplishment of the outstanding ShipAlts and A&I items did not degrade the safety or capability of SCORPION to operate to her restricted depth.

(U) 274. That during SCORPION's 1967 RAV,

    a. All repair work requested was authorized and accomplished.

    b. SCORPION was certified for at sea operations upon completion of RAV by COMSUBRON 6 251939Z Sep 67.

    c. post-availability sea trials were conducted, after which SCORPION returned to the operating piers because the Commanding Officer determined that sea trial deficiencies were so few and minor there was no requirement to return to the shipyard.

(U) 275. That a propeller shaft seal leak was repaired by ORION and satisfactorily tested at sea prior to SCORPION's deployment and that there was no subsequent leakage problem reported by SCORPION.

(U) 276. That on 15 April an open garbage barge being used as a protective fender between SCORPION and USS TALLAHATCHIE COUNTY while moored in Naples, Italy sank due to swamping in heavy weather.

(C)(U) 277. That there is no evidence that a complete underwater body inspection was conducted on SCORPION during the period that she operated in the

CONFIDENTIAL UNCLASSIFIED

(U) (FOUO) 278. That COMSUBRON 6 had on record 109 outstanding work requests in all categories from SCORPION, including all items from her during deployment. COMSUBLANT stated that this number of outstanding items is considered to be less than would normally be expected for a submarine returning from such a deployment. (Exs 45, 110, 111)

(U) 279. That SCORPION had four outstanding CASREPS at the time of her departure from the Mediterranean:

> MK 19 Plotter
> AN/BRA-19 Antenna (AN/BRA-13 tuner portion)
> AN/BRD Antenna
> Main Coolant Outlet Valve Position Indicator (shut position only)

(C)(U) 280. That SCORPION's AN/BRA-19 Telescoping Whip Antenna

    a. operated at the frequency range of [2 to 30 MHz,]

    b. had the same frequency range as the AN/BRA-9 helical antenna,

    c. had an outstanding CASREP stating that the AN/BRA-13 tuner was out of commission, but

    d. remained useable for receiving all transmissions, including LORAN, in the tuner by-pass mode.

(U) 281. That SCORPION had requested an RAV for dry docking, upon her return to Norfolk. The significant work requested was:

    a. painting of hull,

    b. correction of shipyard guarantee items,

    c. selected interim docking routines, and

    d. radiography of non-isolable secondary plant piping.

(C)(U) 282. That, in 1964, a Statement of Operational Requirements (SOR) was issued for the development of a Submarine Emergency Communication Transmitter (SECT). This buoy, for SSBN use only, was to be:

    a. non-tethered,

    b. shock hardened,

    c. manually or automatically releasable, and

    d. [able to transmit two transcribed signals reporting inability to carry out the assigned mission.]

(∅) 283. That, in 1964, an SOR was issued to develop a Submarine Emergency Alerting and Locating Device (SEAL). This buoy, primarily for deep diving submarine use, was to be:

    a. tethered to the submarine,[but automatically released below ⊢ (!) feet.

    b. able to transmit a single prescribed emergency call signal on multiple emergency frequencies, and

    c. installed in the existing messenger buoy space.

(∅)(U) 284. That neither SEAL nor SECT has a requirement to collect and/or transmit ship status data for casualty analysis as is done by the in-flight recorder installed on some airplanes; and that no operational hardware has yet been produced for either project.

(U) 285. That following the USS SCAMP (SSN588) propeller shaft failure in December 1961, SCORPION's main propeller shaft was replaced in January 1962 with a shaft of proven design and manufacture. (Ex 159, 179)

(U) 286. That the Submarine Safety Center, established by SECNAV Notice 5450 of 18 February 1964, and now a part of the Navy Safety Center, Norfolk, has, among other things,

    a. promulgated submarine safety information through Safety Notes, letters, technical reviews, and conferences,

    b. reviewed the SUBSAFE Certification Program, and

    c. recommended expanded efforts in the area of stern plane reliability. (Ex 117)

OPINIONS

(U)   The tragedy of SCORPION's loss will be compounded if any practice, condition or deficiency subject to corrective action and which may have contributed to her loss is not identified and corrected.

(U)   For this reason and because there is no incontrovertible proof of the exact cause or causes for the loss, the Court has addressed itself to corrective measures not only for practices, conditions, and deficiencies associated with the most probable causes of SCORPION's loss, but also to those which were identified with the analyses of less likely causes of her loss.

(S) 1. That the series of acoustic events that occurred about 221844Z May in the vicinity of [L (I)] emanated from SCORPION.

(S) (u) 2. That the first signal of the acoustic event was of a high enough order to indicate a casualty to SCORPION which was cataclysmic in nature.

(S) (u) 3. That there were certain key facts and technical opinions presented to the Court by expert witnesses which are cardinal in estimating the most probable scenario for the loss of SCORPION. These are:

    a. The first recorded acoustic event had a signal strength greater than a 30 pound TNT charge detonated at a depth of 60 feet or more.

    b. There was no bubble pulse recorded with the first acoustic event.

    c. There was a 26 second time interval between events one and two and a 65 second time interval between events two and three.

    d. The remaining events, four through fifteen, were recorded over a time span of 99 seconds.

    e. The position of the first acoustic event was calculated to have occurred west of the other events. This required an easterly movement of SCORPION.

    f. Uncontrollable flooding occurred which filled the hull before reaching pressure hull collapse depth.

    g. The main pressure hull did not collapse into any compartment.

(S) (u) 4. That the acoustic events, one through fifteen, can be accounted for logically by the following scenario:

    a. Uncontrollable flooding was initiated by <u>event number one</u>.

    b. The Engine Room was not damaged by the first event, and was the last compartment to flood.

    c. Propulsion power was maintained until subsequent events destroyed

d. SCORPION took all possible recovery actions, including blowing main ballast tanks, putting rise on all planes, increasing speed, holding an up angle on the ship, but the flooding could not be controlled.

e. SCORPION flooded until the Reactor Compartment or a compartment adjacent thereto, probably the Auxiliary Machinery Space, filled completely.

f. The Reactor Compartment bulkhead(s) collapsed--event number two.

g. SCORPION continued to sink as flooding progressed.

h. The Engine Room bulkhead collapsed--event number three; or, the Torpedo Room bulkhead and Engine Room bulkhead collapsed-- events number three and four.

i. SCORPION was fully flooded before passing hull collapse depth.

j. As SCORPION continued to sink, each intact and unflooded hard tank, trunk, buoy, and torpedo tube imploded as its collapse depth was passed--events four through fifteen.

k. A Graphic Correlation of Collapse Depths with Event Times follows:

(U) 5. That the certain cause for the loss of SCORPION is not ascertainable from any evidence now available.

(U) 6. That it is, however, possible to deduce the most probable of a number of possible causes and to assess the lesser probability of others.

(S) 7. That the most probable cause is based upon a correlation of facts and best evidence available. It is:

a. At about 221844Z there was an acoustic event which was heard and recorded at Argentia [ʰ (1)]

b. When correlated, the data indicated that the approximate position of this event was [ʰ (1)]

c. From her last reported position, a course of 289 degrees and a speed of 15.3 knots would have been required for SCORPION to reach the position of the acoustic event at the time of the event.

d. Both course and speed are compatible with SCORPION's most probable course and speed to make her ETA Norfolk.

e. Allowing time for field day prior to entering port and for the time required to [disarm and] prepare the torpedoes on board for off-loading before entering the Navy Yard for scheduled docking, it would have been highly probable that work had begun on the torpedoes [and may have been in progress at the time of the acoustic event.]

f. Each torpedo warhead had the potential explosive force to give the [indicated] level of energy [of the initial acoustic event] if detonated either inside or outside of the hull.

g. Other than a gas explosion, which is not considered probable, because of the regular checks on atmospheric environment, there was no other single source of sufficiently high potential explosive energy present within the ship.

h. There are ways in which one or more warheads could have been detonated including an uncontrollable fire in the Torpedo Room.

i. Of the ways, it is not possible to determine which one did cause any detonation, [but one which seems to be consistent with the level of training, operating procedures and previous practices is suggested as follows:]

(1) [A Mark 37 torpedo in a tube in fully ready condition, without propeller guard starts a "hot run" due to inadvertent

(3) [Acting on impulse, and perhaps influenced by successful ejection of a Mark 37 exercise shot which was running hot in the tube in December 1967, the torpedo was released from the tube, became fully armed, and sought its nearest target, SCORPION.]

8. That other possible causes are included below in the order of decreasing probability:

FIRE

1. Detonation of a torpedo warhead stowed in the Torpedo Room could be caused by an uncontrolled fire resulting from the ignition of spilled alcohol, spontaneous combustion, or other causes.

2. Upon receiving report of fire in the Torpedo Room, the ship took emergency surfacing action.

3. This fire rapidly became uncontrollable due to the multiplicity of combustible items in the Torpedo Room such as pyrotechnics, torpedo alcohol, torpedo warhead booster charges, dry stores and clothing, and may have been supported and force fed by a ruptured air or oxygen line.

4. One or more torpedo warheads detonated. A high order detonation, although unlikely, would cause severe rupture of the pressure hull boundary and the after bulkhead of the Torpedo Room. The cumulative effect of one or more low order detonations could cause rupture of the pressure hull, torpedo tubes, or torpedo ejection system plus serious injury and death to personnel.

5. As a result of the explosion, ship changed heading for one or a combination of the following reasons:

   a. Gyro tumbled and helmsman attempted to follow repeater swing.

   b. Shock caused rudder malfunctions.

   c. Hull ruptured on one side and drag effect of damage slewed ship around, or the resultant list of the ship caused the stern planes to induce both a rise and turning moment.

WEAPONS HANDLING ACCIDENT

1. SCORPION had some torpedoes in a fully ready condition. Prior to entering port these torpedoes had to be disarmed. SCORPION was scheduled for dry docking shortly after arrival in Norfolk so all of her torpedoes would have to be offloaded.

2. It was SCORPION's practice to schedule evolutions while en route home so as to permit about two days for field day just prior to arrival in Norfolk. Torpedoes would be made ready for offloading during this

3. The procedure normally followed in SCORPION for disarming the warheads of MK-14 torpedoes was to rotate the torpedo sufficiently to allow removal of the exploder mechanism and booster from below the warhead. By this method, the exploder mechanism would be lowered sufficiently to permit a man to get his hand into the exploder cavity of the warhead to catch the booster so that it would not drop out as the exploder mechanism was removed.

4. Although the rather sensitive booster should not detonate from the shock of being dropped a few inches, if from age or by other causes the sensitivity had increased markedly, detonation from shock would be possible.

5. As the exploder was being lowered, the booster was dropped a short distance onto the exploder mechanism and detonated. Being in such close proximity to the warhead cavity, the detonation of the booster caused a high order detonation of the warhead - [b (1)
b (1)   ]

6. As a result of the explosion, ship changed heading for the same reasons as cited above.

COLLISION

1. Collision with a surface warship, merchant ship, or submarine could have caused the loss of SCORPION. Such a collision is considered improbable, however, for the following reasons:

   a. In a search of intelligence there was no information that such a collision occurred nor was there any evidence of any surface ships or submarines in close proximity to SCORPION at the time of the acoustic event]

   b. [While the nature of the acoustic event does not completely rule out the possibility of a collision, it is doubtful that a collision would have generated sufficient acoustic energy to produce a signal of the magnitude of the first event]

   c. Collision with a surface ship during a [classified] submerged transit in the open ocean by a submarine with the relatively high state of training of SCORPION is considered unlikely.

   d. The weather in the vicinity of SCORPION was not severe enough to cause depth control problems to a trained crew at periscope or communication depth. Even if there were a collision with a surface ship the damage to SCORPION would in all probability be limited to the sail area. Only an extremely deep draft surface ship could fatally contact the pressure hull of SCORPION while submerged. A large

e. If a collision with a surface ship occurred and the surface ship sank immediately, some debris or survivors would have had a high probability of being discovered during the intensive search for SCORPION.

2. Collision with a sea mount could have caused the loss of SCORPION. It is considered unlikely that this happened for the following reasons:

a. SCORPION was probably transiting at a depth of less than 300 feet.

b. SCORPION's navigation accuracy was such that she probably had fixed her position [within two or three miles.]

c. Extensive bottom surveys conducted subsequent to the loss have revealed no soundings less than 128 fathoms along or near the probable track of SCORPION.

d. [The nature of the first signal and timing of the subsequent signals of the acoustic event were such that it is doubtful that they could have been caused by collision with a sea mount.]

(S)

FOUL PLAY (SABOTAGE)

1. The possibility of foul play was considered, particularly in view of the unexplained losses of the Israeli and French submarines in the Mediterranean where SCORPION had so recently been operating. Among other possibilities these were examined:

a. An explosive device attached to the hull, internally or externally, which ruptured the hull.

b. An explosive device attached to a torpedo which detonated the warhead.

c. A safety device, such as a torpedo tube door interlock, which might have been tampered with.

2. The probability of any of these occurrences is evaluated as very low. [A small charge such as a limpet mine could not have been heard at the Argentia hydrophones. A charge of at least 30 pounds in water would have been required to record the first acoustic event. It is most unlikely that a swimmer would use a charge of that size, particularly when he could have done the job with a [b(1)]] The intrusion of a saboteur on board SCORPION is remote in view of the security provisions in nuclear submarines. The skill and time required to sabotage a safety device makes that possibility even more remote. To all this can be added the fact that 25 days elapsed between leaving port and the acoustic event.]

time or gave any other sign that they had knowledge of SCORPION's
loss, as they did in other [somewhat similar situations.] While the
Soviets are not necessarily advised of all acts [of sabotage,]
this is still another indicator which reduced the probability of
[sabotage.]

(FOUO) (U) IRRATIONAL ACT

1. The Court considered the possibility that an irrational act by a
member of the ship's company might have caused the loss of SCORPION
and assessed the probability as remote.

2. An act such as a bullet fired into a torpedo warhead could have
caused an explosion, but there is no evidence that any member of the
ship's company was suffering from or had ever suffered from
psychiatric illness. On the contrary, there is positive evidence
that this was a group of men marked by maturity and mental
stability.

(S) FLOODING DUE TO STRUCTURAL FAILURE OR PERSONNEL ERROR

1. Depending on the depth, speed and size of opening, flooding due to
structural failure or personnel error could have caused the loss of
SCORPION. However, it is considered unlikely that this type of
casualty directly caused the loss for the following reasons:

   a. The ship would have been operating at less than 300 feet keel
   depth. She had routinely operated at deeper depths and
   structural failure is not likely to have occurred at the
   shallower depth.

   b. SCORPION was considered fully capable of operation down to her
   authorized depth [of ᴸ⁽ⁱ⁾ feet] (and recently she had so
   operated). Her flooding recovery capability was excellent.
   No SUBSAFE items or alterations which affected safe operation
   down to ᴸ⁽ⁱ⁾ feet were uncompleted.

   c. Operating procedures in SCORPION conformed to the "Guidance
   and Considerations with regard to Submerged Operations"
   promulgated by the Submarine Type Commanders in respect to
   recoverability from flooding and control surface failure.

   d. The ship was at the end of a deployment and the state of
   training, at least for routine operations such as a transit,
   could be expected to be at a high level.

   e. [Even had flooding occurred in a location such as to cause
   immediate loss of reactor power, residual heat in the reactor
   plant would enable the ship to propel itself at about ten
   knots for about [ᴸ⁽ⁱ⁾] minutes, or at higher speeds for

the ship should have been capable of recovering from a hole size of about ⌊(l)⌋ inches diameter. The only ⌈sea water⌉ system as large as ⌊(l)⌋ inches is the ⌈main sea water⌉ system which is constructed and tested to the designed collapse depth of the ship. Other possible openings of large size are the torpedo tubes, snorkel system, main shaft, secondary propulsion motor shaft, trash disposal unit, and penetrating masts. None of these are considered likely as causes of serious flooding.

g. ⌈The initiation of a flooding casualty due to structural failure or personnel error would not generate sufficient energy to produce an acoustic event of the magnitude of the first event recorded⌋

(S)

LOSS OF SHIP CONTROL

1. It is possible that the loss of SCORPION was caused by loss of ship control which resulted in her exceeding her collapse depth. Loss of ship control could have been precipitated by a hydraulic or mechanical failure in the stern plane control system and aggravated by a delay in the initiation of recovery action by the ship control party.

2. Although the foregoing is possible, it is considered improbable because:

   a. During her transit SCORPION was probably operating at speeds up to ⌊(l)⌋ knots and at depths no greater than 300 feet.

   b. Stern plane jam studies conducted by NSRDC show that if the stern planes jammed on full dive at 300 feet and ⌊(l)⌋ knots, SCORPION, through the use of emergency backing, full rise on the sail planes and her normal main ballast tank blow system, could recover without exceeding her collapse depth even after a time delay of 12 seconds in initiating recovery action. This 12 seconds delay is in addition to the nine seconds delay for human reaction and manipulation times already incorporated into the recovery studies.

   c. SCORPION's crew was experienced and members of the ship control party were required to complete a detailed training program in order to qualify for the watch station assigned. Casualty training and drills were conducted for all watchstanders.

   d. SCORPION had experienced stern plane failures to full dive and plane control was regained in the emergency mode in each instance subsequent to the modification of the stern plane control system in 1961.

   e. The pitch angle that SCORPION would most likely reach by the time the stern planes reached full dive would ensure a very

~~SECRET~~

f. The stern plane system in SCORPION's class has a high degree of mechanical and electrical reliability and is the standard for reliability when making a design review for other class submarines.

g. If SCORPION had exceeded her crush depth because of loss of ship control, the initial acoustic event would have been caused by implosion of the hull and would have been followed within very few seconds by a series of higher frequency pulses caused by collapsing bulkheads and tank implosions. In addition, implosion of the hull at crush depth would in all probability create a discernable bubble pulse frequency. A bubble pulse was not observed as the first pulse of the actual event and the total pattern and timing between events would be significantly different in an implosion at crush depth than the signals recorded on the [b (1)] on 22 May.

(U)   9. That it is improbable that the loss of SCORPION was caused by sabotage or was the result of enemy action.

(U) 10. That it is highly improbable that the loss of SCORPION was due to the irrational act of any individual.

(U) 11. That the weather which would have been encountered by SCORPION along her prescribed track would not have been of sufficient severity to endanger a submarine of her class.

(U) 12. That a timely and effective air, surface, and sub-surface search for SCORPION was conducted.

(U) 13. That SCORPION was effectively manned, enjoyed reasonably good personnel stability, and that her officers and crew were well trained.

(U) 14. That enhanced ship control safety would be provided if separate Diving Officer of the Watch and Chief of the Watch (Ballast Control Panel Operator) were assigned whenever submerged.

~~(C)~~ (U) 15. That the relative inexperience displayed by Commander Slattery in the submarine versus submarine role in January 1968 was not prejudicial to his ability to effectively handle his ship in other tactical situations, and did not reflect on his ability to make a safe transit.

(U) ~~(FOUO)~~ 16. That the policy of the Commanders of the Submarine Forces with respect to the PCO School is sound. It does not, however, make adequate provisions for PCO's who, through the exigencies of scheduling, may need tactical updating in any particular facet of submarine warfare.

(U) 17. That the Commanding Officer of SCORPION was mindful for the safety of

(U)   18.   That the Navigator and navigation personnel attached to and serving
              in SCORPION were capable of safely navigating the ship.

(U)   19.   That the navigation equipment installed in SCORPION was adequate to
              safely navigate the ship and that none of the reported navigation
              equipment malfunctions would have jeopardized safe navigation.

(U)   20.   That although it could not be positively established whether or not
              LORAN A Chart VL 30-24 was on board, the fact that SCORPION
              obtained similar charts adjacent on either side of it from CANOPUS
              and a supply of chart VL 30-24 was available at the same time
              indicates that SCORPION probably had this chart on board.

(C)   21.   That during the transit, SCORPION was most probably operating at
              speeds no greater than x_0 knots and at depths no greater than 300
              feet.

(U)   22.   That Lieutenant Commander Stephens was a prudent navigator and as
              such could be expected to obtain all available charts that would
              pertain to SCORPION's operation.

(U)   23.   That faulty navigation was not the proximate cause of the loss of
              SCORPION.

(U)   24.   That the results of surveys conducted in the vicinity of Hyeres Bank
              and Cruiser Sea Mount and along SCORPION's prescribed track show it
              to be unlikely that she collided with an undiscovered sea mount.

(U) (FOUO) 25.   That the bottom contour charts presently issued for general use are
              not of sufficient accuracy or detail to permit safe submerged
              navigation in all areas where U. S. submarines operate.

(U)   26.   That as the speed, depth, and long submergence capabilities of
              submarines are increased the danger of submerged collisions with
              uncharted sea mounts will increase.

(U)   27.   That the present piecemeal correction of inaccurate bottom contour
              navigation charts is not the solution to this dangerous situation.

(U)   28.   That, if a stern plane jam on full dive occurred, SCORPION would
              have recognized the casualty within 10 seconds and would have
              taken recovery action.

(U)   29.   That based on recoverability from flooding and from stern plane
              casualties, the 18 knot SOA prescribed for SCORPION's transit from
              south of the Azores to Norfolk is not considered excessive.

(U)   30.   That there is no identifiable pattern of casualties which affect
              the safe operation of the SSN 588 Class submarines.

UNCLASSIFIED

(U) 32. That COMSUBLANT/COMSUBPAC Joint Instruction 03120.9A/03120.15A, Subject: "Guidance and Considerations with regard to Submerged Operations," provides excellent guidance and was generally followed by SCORPION.

(U) 33. That, had SCORPION received the messages transmitted to her on 23, 24, and 25 May which requested replies, she would have been justified in not responding to them since the operation order under which she was operating specified electronic silence.

(U) 34. That the sinking of the barge between SCORPION and TALLAHATCHIE COUNTY on 15 April did not cause damage to SCORPION or contribute to her subsequent loss.

(U) 35. That significant advances have been made in the development of diving trainers and their usefulness is recognized in the Submarine Force.

(C) 36. That the inoperative [⌐ 𝓁 (1)   ⌐] valve shut position indicator] would not affect reactor safety because it is not a part of the reactor protective circuitry and other indications are available[⌐ 𝓁 (1)   ⌐]

(U) (FOUO) 37. That the oxygen candle furnace is a potential fire hazard.

(U) (FOUO) 38. That persons who have been disqualified for submarine duty as a result of a psychiatric evaluation should not be permitted to return to duty in submarines.

(U) (C) 39. [That it is possible for an explosive charge to detonate against the hull of a submarine, vent into the hull and not create a bubble pulse.]

(U) (C) 40. That between about 170001Z May and the time of her loss SCORPION had some torpedoes [in a fully ready condition.]

(U) 41. That subsequent to transmitting her position and ETA message (212354Z May) SCORPION would have been preparing torpedoes for off-loading upon arrival in Norfolk.

(U) (FOUO) 42. That the use of standard check lists from NAVWEPS publications enhances torpedo safety and should be available for all shipboard evolutions performed on torpedoes in service use.

(U) 43. That the extensive SUBSAFE work accomplished at Charleston Naval Shipyard during the 1963-64 RO significantly upgraded the material condition of SCORPION and enhanced her operational safety.

(U) 44. That the SUBSAFE program has resulted in significant improvements in the ability of high performance submarines to operate more safely at deep depth and that continued emphasis to assure full consideration of future developments is warranted.

(U)   46.   That the SUBSAFE program has been delayed by the limitation of industrial capacities and capabilities.

(U)   47.   That the normal main ballast tank blow system installed in SCORPION was operating satisfactorily.

(U)   48.   That the lack of an operable EMBT blow system did not constitute a safety hazard for operation of SCORPION to her restricted depth and did not contribute to her loss.

(U)   49.   That the operation of deep diving submarines to their restricted depth is safe, in so far as the material condition is concerned, without the accomplishment of SUBSAFE alterations, but, obviously, safety is enhanced by each SUBSAFE alteration completed.

(U)   50.   That the loss of SCORPION is not attributed to the delayed completion of her full SUBSAFE program.

(U)   51.   That the Submarine Safety Center has been an effective instrument for the dissemination of information, the review of requirements, and has made a significant contribution to the safe operation of submarines.

(U)   52.   That the pressure hull of SCORPION was sound and operationally safe for the depth to which she was restricted.

(U)   53.   That there are no known or suspected pressure hull deficiencies that contributed to the loss of SCORPION.

(U) (FOUO)   54.   That there is inadequate technical data available to predict the effects of internal explosions on personnel and structures.

(U)   55.   That, while SCORPION's hydraulic systems were a continuing upkeep and maintenance item, there was no history of extensive salt water contamination and the problems and casualties experienced were not unique, unusual, or indicative of unsound or unsafe ship control hydraulic systems.

(U) (FOUO)   56.   That, while there is no direct evidence that SCORPION was lost as a result of a stern plane failure, the stern plane control system constitutes one of the most potentially hazardous systems affecting the safe operation of high speed nuclear submarines.

(U)   57.   That hydraulic system cleanliness is important to the reliable operation of these systems.

(U) (C)   58.   That the lack of data for stern plane action and failure position when "cast free", hydraulically or mechanically, constitutes an information void for design considerations that could affect submarine safety.

(U) (FOUO) 60. That the hydraulic power plant design for the SSN585/588 Class has a high degree of mechanical and electrical reliability but the system is subject to simultaneous failure of all pumps due to salt water spray.

(U) 61. That SCORPION's hydraulic power steering and diving control systems were operating satisfactorily and did not constitute an undue hazard for safe operations.

(U) 62. That the propeller shaft and shaft seal installed in SCORPION were sound and did not contribute to the loss of SCORPION.

(U) 63. That SCORPION had adequate capability to transmit and receive radio communications.

(U) 64. That Freon-12 did not contribute to the loss of SCORPION.

(U) 65. That, while the oxygen system is one of the potentially hazardous systems installed, SCORPION's oxygen system was:

   a. properly constructed, maintained and operated

   b. trouble-free and virtually impossible to contaminate if a positive pressure was maintained

   c. arranged such that the probability of damaging the system inadvertently was remote.

(U) 66. That the oxygen system was not the primary cause of SCORPION's loss.

(U) (C) 67. That, on high performance, deep diving, nuclear submarines, there is a need for a recoverable data recording system which will facilitate casualty analysis, and will be compatible with submarine military characteristics.

(U) (FOUO) 68. That, in view of the low flash point of ethyl alcohol and the presence of combustibles in the torpedo room, the potential for a serious alcohol fire exists.

(U) 69. That the probability of a major explosion of hydrogen gas from the main storage battery is very low and, even if it should occur, lethel damage to the pressure hull is improbable from such an explosion.

(U) 70. That the probability of an uncontrollable fire being initiated by a hydraulic leak is very low.

(U) (FOUO) 71. That, while SCORPION had four CASREPS and 109 work requests outstanding, none of these were of a nature that would affect safe operation of the ship.

(U) (FOUO) 72. That SCORPION's overall material condition was excellent and none of the outstanding ship alterations or incomplete A&I items were required for safe operation to her restricted depth.

(U)   73.   That no radiological hazard resulted from the loss of SCORPION.

(U)   74.   That the evidence does not establish that the loss of SCORPION and deaths of those embarked were caused by the intent, fault, negligence or inefficiency of any person or persons in the Naval service or connected therewith.

(FOUO)   Although the Court has not been able to determine the exact cause of the loss of SCORPION, the evidence adduced in this inquiry and the findings therefrom have disclosed certain possible indirect and contributing conditions which, in the interest of preventing other such losses, warrant further in-depth study and consideration.

Certain of those conditions have been highlighted in the operational and material areas. Associated with these are probable personnel errors. As is so often the case, it is more difficult to assess the root causes for personnel errors since they may be attributable to any combination of:

a. inadequate training,

b. inexperience,

c. lack of proper motivation,

d. carelessness, or

e. unpredictable reactions to emergencies.

With particular regard to officers serving in modern high performance submarines an evaluation of the evidence indicates that there may be a need for some additional emphasis on the essential tactical skills necessary for the exercise of command.

While the Court fully appreciates the need for technical and management expertise, it is of the opinion that of equal importance is the need to insure that those essential skills and tactical experience required of a sea going officer to safely and effectively operate these complex ships are maintained in a proper balance such that those officers who achieve command will be prepared to effectively exercise all of the functions of command.

RECOMMENDATIONS

(U)   1.   That action be taken on a priority basis to increase the coverage of accurate bathymetric information available to submarines, using the most modern navigation and sounding systems available.

(U)   2.   That NAVOCEANO's proposed system of Notices to Submerged Mariners be implemented and expanded to include information from all sources and be disseminated to all submarines.

(U)   3.   That a satellite navigation system be installed on all high performance submarines.

4.   That, to enhance the submerged navigational ability and to provide increased safety from submerged groundings, all high speed SSNs be provided with a [secure sounding device]

(U) (FOUO)   5.   That operational commanders insure that appropriate consideration be given to all information available on navigational hazards and navigational aids when prescribing routes for submarine transits.

(U)   6.   That responsible commanders give consideration to a requirement for [complete underwater hull inspections] of all submarines prior to their getting underway from any foreign port.

(U) (FOUO)   7.   That consideration be given to establishing a policy preventing persons once disqualified for psychiatric reasons, from again serving in submarines.

(U) (FOUO)   8.   That consideration be given to establishing a program to foster the tactical updating of officers prior to assuming command.

(U)   9.   That, in any changes in the organization for safety in the Navy, care be taken to ensure the continued effectiveness of the former Submarine Safety Center in promoting greater safety in the construction, maintenance, and operation of submarines.

(U) (FOUO)   10.   That consideration be given to the development of factual data on the effects of explosions inside of a submarine on personnel, equipments, and structures to provide guidance for future improvements.

(U) (FOUO)   11.   That the continuing program for upgrading stern planes reliability receive high management attention and emphasis in the technical and operational commands.

(U) (FOUO)   12.   That means for shipboard maintenance of hydraulic systems cleanliness and improved protection against salt water spray damage be considered for inclusion in the program for upgrading stern plane reliability.

(C) (U) 13. That hydrodynamic studies and tests be made to determine the resultant effects of stern planes being "cast free."

(U) (FOUO) 14. That consideration be given to the conduct of a study by the Navy Safety Center of the danger of fires aboard submarines. Such a study should include, but not be limited to:

    a. Identifying potential hazards.

    b. Increasing the information available to submarines regarding fire hazards.

    c. Reviewing the adequacy of firefighting equipments provided.

    d. Reviewing procedures for combating fires in submarines.

    e. Investigating stowage arrangements.

    f. Investigating areas where additional protective equipments may be warranted.

    g. Investigating special firefighting equipment to blanket or smother fires.

    h. Improving fire resistance of materials.

(U) (FOUO) 15. That oxygen candle furnaces be operated in areas remote from explosives and highly flammable materials.

(U) (FOUO) 16. That consideration be given to reemphasizing safety precautions and emergency procedures for torpedoes, with particular emphasis on "hot runs" of fully ready tactical weapons.

(U) (FOUO) 17. That consideration be given to determining the adequacy and availability of complete and accurate check lists for all torpedoes and to insure that those lists are properly used.

(U) (FOUO) 18. That consideration be given to modifying the propeller guard of MK 37 torpedoes to provide a positive lock of the [fin velocity switch] to prevent inadvertent operation.

Vice Admiral, U. S. Navy (Retired)
President

Rear Admiral, U. S. Navy
Member

Captain, U. S. Navy
Member

Captain, U. S. Navy
Member

Captain, U. S. Navy
Member

Captain, U. S. Navy
Member

Commander, U. S. Navy
Member

Final entry.

Vice Admiral, U. S. Navy (Retired)
President

Congress of the United States

JOINT COMMITTEE ON ATOMIC ENERGY

WASHINGTON, D.C. 20510

July 24, 1968

Honorable
Secretary of the Navy
Department of the Navy
Washington, D. C. 20350

Dear Mr. Secretary:

On behalf of the Joint Committee, I wish to thank you for the
assistance and cooperation provided by your office, the Office of
the Chief of Naval Operations, the Commander in Chief, U. S.
Atlantic Fleet and the Commander, Submarine Force, U. S. Atlantic
Fleet in arranging for and accommodating an observer from the
Joint Committee staff at the search headquarters and at the court
of inquiry concerning the tragic loss of USS SCORPION.

It is my understanding that the court of inquiry upon completion of its investigation into the loss of the USS SCORPION will
submit its record of proceedings together with findings of fact,
opinions and recommendations to the Commander in Chief, U. S.
Atlantic Fleet, the convening authority.

It would be appreciated if a copy of the proceedings, together
with the findings of fact, opinions and recommendations of the court
of inquiry, and the action of the convening authority be furnished to
the Joint Committee on Atomic Energy as soon as practicable after
the convening authority has acted.

Sincerely yours,

B6 -

Chairman

000335

2 7390

1 AUG 1968

My dear Mr. Chairman:

I have received your letter of July 24, 1968 requesting a copy of
the record of proceedings of the Court of Inquiry relating to the
loss of USS SCORPION, together with the findings of fact, opinions
and recommendations of the Court and the action thereon of the
convening authority.

The convening authority, Commander in Chief, U. S. Atlantic Fleet,
has not yet completed his review of and action on the record. When
this has been done and the record has been received, I shall advise
you promptly.

Please be assured of my desire to cooperate with you fully in this
matter.

Sincerely,

Secretary of the Navy

Honorable
Chairman, Joint Committee on Atomic Energy
United States Senate
Washington, D. C. 20510

ALL B6

U.S.S. SCORPION (SSN 589)
CARE OF FLEET POST OFFICE
NEW YORK, NEW YORK 09501

SSN589:RRF:lw
9000
27 November 1967

MEMORANDUM

From: Commanding Officer, USS SCORPION (SSN589)
To: Commander Submarine Squadron SIX

Subj: Background Information on SCORPION Vibration at High Speed

February 1967 - SCORPION drydocked at NNSY. Propeller and shaft were removed for replacement of shaft sleeve in way of sealol seal. Sealol seals and inflatable boot replaced. Visual inspection of shaft, bearings and propeller showed no defects. While in the shop for replacement of the sleeve, the shaft was dropped. No damage was observed.

April 1967 - Shaft was reinstalled in ship. After reinstallation it was found that the sealol seal was improperly installed. This required re-pulling of the shaft to correct the sealol seal installation.

May 1967 - A correct fit per plan could not be obtained during reinstallation of the propeller. After design consultation it was confirmed that the shaft taper was indeed according to plan. Therefore the propeller hub was rebored to match the taper of the shaft. Subsequent reinstallation was satisfactory.

September 1967 - Sea trials were conducted after sitting in wet dock at NNSY for 4 months. Excessive propeller cavitation, coupled with the loss of almost 2 knots at full power from pre-yard experience was observed. On return from trials the propeller and underwater body were inspected by ORION divers, who reported no significant fouling and no damage to the screw.

October 1967 - Enroute to New London for REFTRA the same excessive cavitation and loss of speed were observed. Inspection by SUBASE divers was requested. They reported heavy fouling of the propeller, but scraped off most of the excess. SCORPION was later drydocked in ARD-7 for repairs to #6 torpedo tube stop bolt housing. At this time ship's force and SUBASE propeller shop personnel polished the screw and sharpened the blade edges. One gouge about 4 inches long by one-sixteenth inch maximum depth in the face of one blade was found after the propeller was cleaned. No other defects were observed. The rope guard was removed and a double handful of guidance wire was removed from around the shaft. There was no evidence on careful visual inspection of any wire in the stern tube bearing.

SSN589;RRF;lw
27 November 1967

November 1967 - During the transit and ISE period from New London to Bermuda the ship was again operated at high speed. It was observed that cavitation was still in excess of the ship's pre-yard cavitation curve, but that full speed capability had been regained (a 2 knot increase). No abnormal vibration was observed. During the transit from Bermuda to Roosevelt Roads [redacted] the ship refrained from high speed operation.

November 1967 - On 15 November, a week after arrival in Roosevelt Roads and after the firing of [redacted] torpedoes had been completed, the ship transitted to St. Croix, Virgin Islands. During this transit it was observed the ship was still capable of speed in excess of [redacted] knots, but that a heavy vibration of the ship occurred at speeds greater than about [redacted] knots. Above [redacted] knots the vibration appeared to diminish slightly. The frequency of this vibration was synchronous with shaft RPM. The nature of the vibration was similar to that of a washing machine with an unbalanced load. It was observed that there was a slight "hunting" of the rudder ram. However, readjustment of the [redacted] dither voltage to the control valve eliminated this "hunting" with little effect upon the vibration. AFWR divers inspected the screw in St. Croix and reported no damage.

On 18 November the ship returned to Roosevelt Roads, observing the same phenomenon enroute. On arrival divers again inspected the propeller, and removed a small amount of [redacted] wire from the rope guard. They also entered the "mud tank", the free-flooding after portion of the ship surrounding the shaft and rudder and stern plane mechanisms. They found no indication in this area as to the source of vibration. On 19 November the ship again operated at flank speed, and ascertained vibration was still observed at speeds greater than [redacted] knots. For this reason a previously planned full power run enroute to Norfolk was cancelled, and ship speed was limited to [redacted] knots or less on the return voyage.

Very respectfully,

F. A. SLATTERY

Note:

Supplemental information will be provided after ORION divers become available to conduct systematic inspection of stern area.

C.O. opinion is that the vibration is shaft bearing related. This opinion is based on the fact that relocating the point of maximum pressure between shaft and bearing will induce a vibration at almost any speed. For instance, a hard rudder turn causes the ship to heel, which in turn induces a vibration. The vibration is not precisely the same

RECORD OF ORAL OR TELEPHONIC CONVERSATION
NAVEC NORVA

SS(N)-589/9430
Ser 6003-907

1 9 DEC 1967

Project No: SS(N)-589   Date: Week of 11 December 1967

Medium: Oral & Telephone

Initiated by: Ship's force

With: R. R. Padden (NAVEC)

Subject: USS SCAMPION (SS(N)-589)

Equip/Type: Main Propulsion Shafting

Resume:

1. Problems with shafts and hull vibration were discussed with various members of the ship's force during the week of 11 December 1967. The ship complained of occasional severe vibration of the after section of the hull at what was thought to be once per shaft revolution and NAVSECNORDIV was requested to investigate.

2. Subsequent to the initial inquiry work was done on the main hydraulic system and the system was purged. No difficulty was experienced after above repairs.

3. Further investigation will be held in abeyance pending evaluation of the effect of recent work.

Action taken:

Noted for file.

R. R. PADDEN
HEAD   NAVEC

Encl. ( ) to _____ Ser 66_____

NAVAL SPEEDLETTER

FOR URGENT LETTERS ONLY

DO NOT CLEAR THROUGH COMMUNICATION OFFICE

(One box must be checked)

☐ REGULAR MAIL   ☐ SPECIAL DELIVERY
HAND CARRY
☐ REGISTERED GUARD MAIL   ☐ REGISTERED MAIL

CLASSIFICATION
DECLASSIFIED

IN REPLY REFER TO
AS18;ll:ajf
9000
Ser 01556

DATE
5 DEC 1967

TO:
Commander
Submarine Squadron SIX
FPO New York 09501

NAVAL SPEEDLETTER—

Permits dispatch or informal language.

May be sent (1) with enclosures, (2) in a window envelope (size 6⅞" x 3⅝"), if contents are not classified as confidential or higher, (3) to both naval and nonnaval activities.

(Fold)

An underwater hull inspection was conducted on USS SCORPION (SSN589) to determine cause of stern vibration. The inspection was completed on 1 December 1967 with the following results:

Visual inspection, by four different divers, of the entire afterbody, revealed no visible cause for vibration.

One section of the propeller rope guard was removed and a dial indicator installed on the bearing housing. The shaft was then rotated two complete revolutions with no visible runout.

Inspection of propeller indicated no external damage or possible cause of vibration.

J. C. BELLAH

COPY TO

CO, USS SCORPION (SSN589)

ADDRESS
Commanding Officer
U.S.S. ORION (AS18)
FPO New York 09501

SENDER'S MAILING ADDRESS

Address reply as shown at left; or reply hereon and return in window envelope (size 6⅞" x 3⅝"), if not classified as confidential or higher.

CLASSIFICATION
DECLASSIFIED

FCSS6/41:egm
9400
Ser 0356
5 DEC 1967

From: Commander Submarine Squadron SIX
To: Commander Submarine Force, U. S. Atlantic Fleet

Subj: USS SCORPION (SSN589) High Speed Vibration; request for technical assistance on

Encl: (1) CO, USS ORION (AS18) spdltr 9000 ser 01556 of 5 DEC 67

1. Since completion of planned restricted availability at Norfolk Naval Shipyard in October 1967, SCORPION has experienced excessive cavitation progressing to heavy vibration at high speeds. This letter reviews the background and concludes with a request for technical assistance.

2. A brief history of work accomplished, problems encountered and steps taken to determine the cause are as follows:

   a. During RAV shaft and propeller were removed for sealol seal replacement. During reassembly a correct fit could not be obtained between the shaft and propeller. Shipyard design confirmed proper shaft taper and the propeller hub was rebored to match the taper of the shaft. Rudder and stern plane readings were within specifications on completion of routine inspection.

   b. On sea trials following RAV in September 1967, propeller cavitation was in excess of pre-RAV cavitation curve coupled with a loss of two knots at full power from pre-yard experience. Inspection by divers on return to port revealed no significant underwater fouling or damage to the screw.

   c. While in New London for REFTRA, SCORPION was dry docked in ARD-7 for repairs to #6 torpedo tube stopbolt housing. At that time SUB BASE propeller shop polished the screw and sharpened the blade edges. One gouge four inches long by one-sixteenth of an inch deep was the only propeller defect noted. Some torpedo guidance wire was removed from around the shaft on removal of rope guards. There was no evidence of wire in the stern tube bearing.

   d. Subsequent to REFTRA a transit was made from New London to Bermuda. Cavitation was still in excess of ships cavitation curve, however, SCORPION full power speed increased two knots to that attained prior to TAV. No abnormal vibration was observed.

FCSS6/41:egm
9400

e. An opposed transit was made from Bermuda to Roosevelt Roads and high-speed operations were not conducted. SCORPION operated one week at Roosevelt Roads, firing mines and non-wire guided torpedoes and departed for St. Croix on 15 November 1967. During the transit full power capability did not change, however, heavy shaft vibration developed at about ▢▢ knots. The vibration diminished slightly above ▢▢▢ knots. The nature of the vibration was similar to a washing machine with an unbalanced load and synchronous with shaft RPM. Visual inspection of divers at St. Croix revealed no screw damage.

f. SCORPION returned to Roosevelt Roads 18 November 1967 noting no change from conditions in paragraph 1.e. At Roosevelt Roads another underwater inspection was made including entering the free flooding area surrounding the shaft, rudder and stern plane mechanisms. A small amount of torpedo guidance wire was removed from the rope guard. The inspection revealed no other abnormal conditions that might contribute to the heavy vibration.

g. On 19 November SCORPION operated at flank speed noting the same conditions reported in paragraph 1.e.

h. SCORPION's speed was held below ▢▢▢▢ knots on her return voyage to Norfolk. A visual inspection of SCORPION's entire afterbody completed 1 December by four different divers, as reported in enclosure (1), revealed no visible cause for vibration. Dial indicator readings taken by the divers from the shaft bearing housing to the shaft showed no discernable shaft run-out. Feeler gauge readings between the shaft and external bearing are within specifications.

3. Commanding Officer, USS SCORPION (SSN589) has been directed to avoid operating in the critical vibration speed range except in emergency conditions.

4. In view of critical forthcoming operations assigned to SCORPION, it is requested that technical assistance be obtained from Naval Ships Systems Engineering Command to conduct onboard inspection and tests inport and underway to determine the cause of excessive vibration and recommend a course of corrective action in order that timely repairs may be made to enable SCORPION to meet her commitments.

J. E. CLARKE, III

2

HIGH-SPEED VIBRATION PROBLEM

Having undergone thorough inspection alongside Pier 22, Norfolk by
ORION, Squadron and NAVSEC NORVA Division personnel - which disclosed no
reason for the vibration - SCORPION got underway on 4 December for
scheduled operations. The Commanding Officer had been directed by
COMSUBRON SIX to not exceed [ ] knots in view of the undetermined vibration
problem.

During this underway period of 4-8 December 1967, SCORPION operated at
all speeds up to [ ] knots. At the direction of the embarked Division
Commander, COMSUBDIV 62, speed was increased in steps to flank. The
ship's performance was observed by ship's company, the Division Commander,
and the Squadron Engineer (also embarked) to be normal. Vibration at
flank speed and other high speeds was considered to be normal for this
ship and class. Acoustic takes were recorded and sent to [ ]
[ ], at the Submarine Base New London, for analysis; however, it
was expected that the results of his analysis would be inconclusive since
the excess vibration was no longer present.

The only physical phenomenon noted as possibly abnormal was a very
small (about - [ ]), low frequency (about [ ]) oscillation of the
rudder ram. This would probably originate in the servo-control loop for
the rudder, and may have been caused by small quantities of air in the
hydraulic servo-control valve.

The cause of the originally reported vibration remains unknown. Since
the ship reported that the hydraulic system had been vented on several
occasions since the vibration appeared, it is considered likely that air
in the system had affected the servo-loops of the rudder, stern planes, or
both, causing the control surfaces to move. In particular, if the surfaces
were caused to oscillate at a frequency corresponding to one of the
natural vibration frequencies of the hull, a noticeable hull vibration
could be expected to result.

[ ]

COMSUBRON SIX Engineer

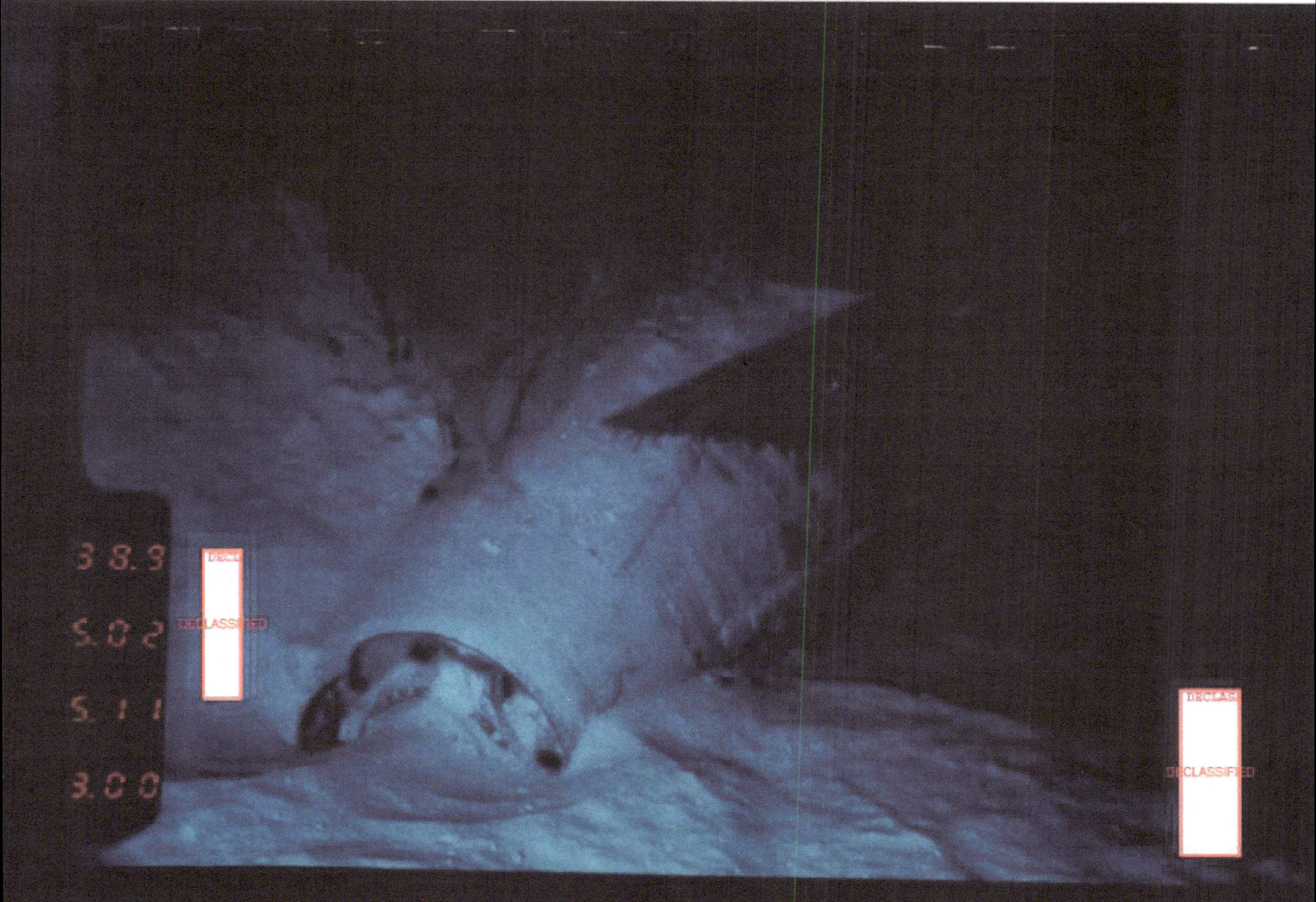
38.9
5.02
5.11
3.00
DECLASSIFIED

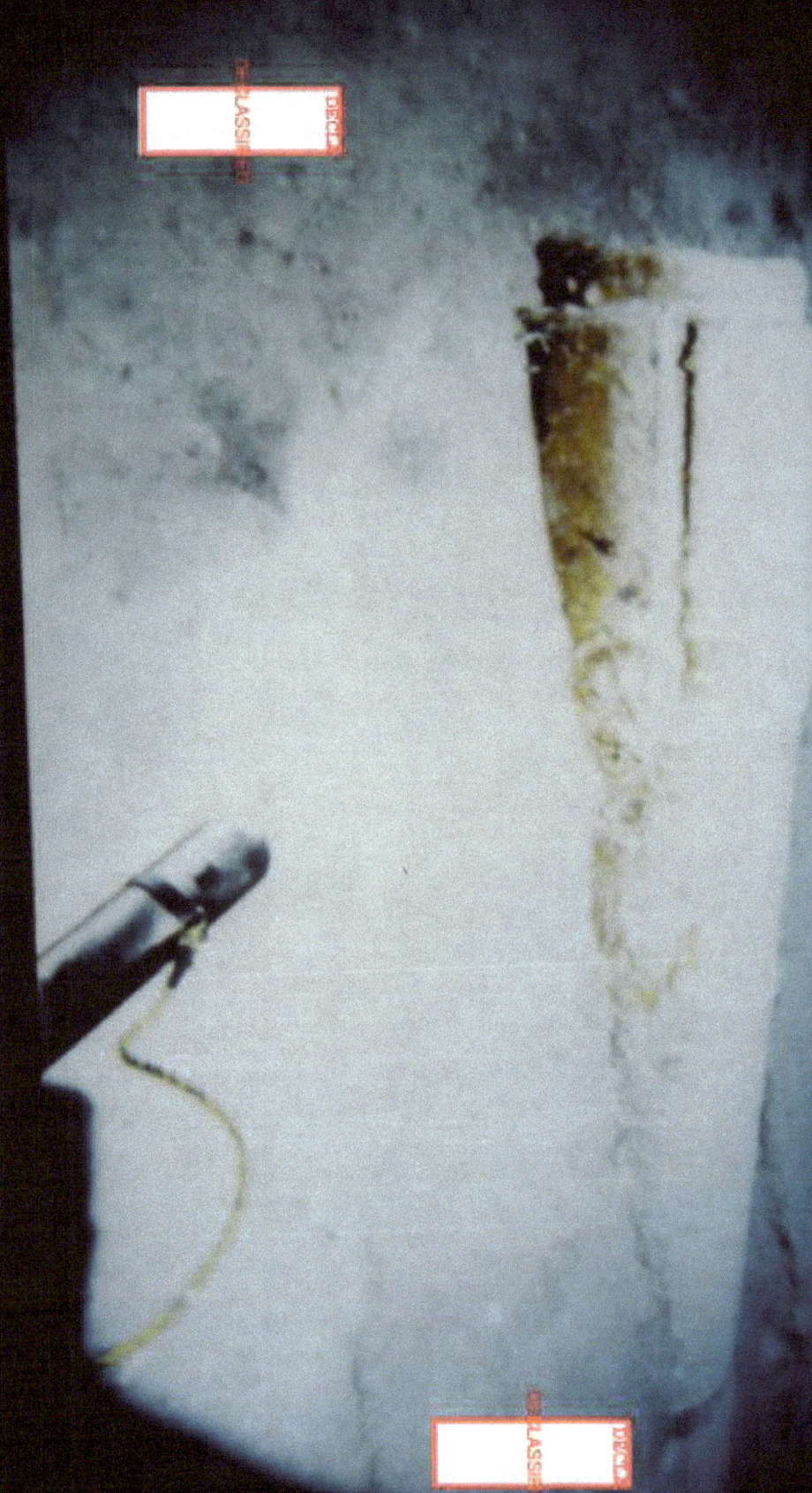

6

PROPELLER

Declassified per OPNAVINST 5513.16B on 13Jun 2012

Declassified by OPNAV N97

FIG 1

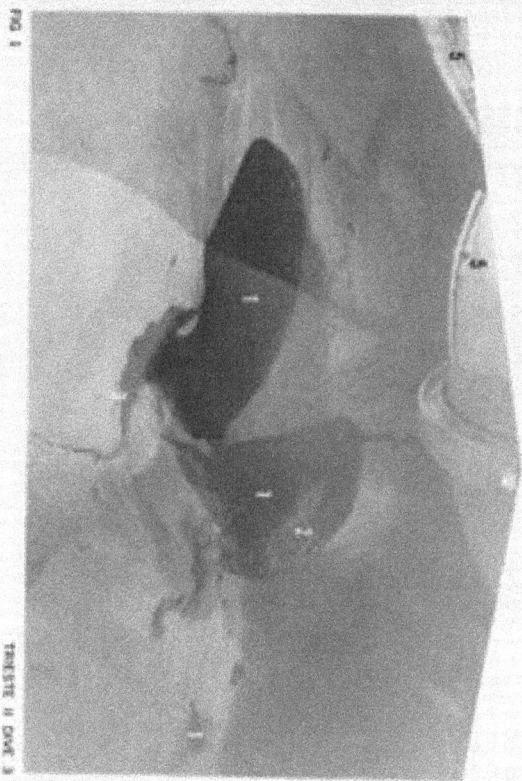

TRIESTE II DIVE 3

FIGURE 1 is a mosaic compiled from TRIESTE II photography showing two blades and the tip of a third blade of a seven-blade propeller. The pressure sphere of TRIESTE II is also visible.

FIGURE 2 is a stereo triplicate showing the scratched or abraded area of the visible blade. The sharp edge of the crater over the hub of the propeller is also visible.

FIGURE 3, taken by MIZAR, shows the propeller with attached shaft and several pieces of miscellaneous debris.

ANNOTATIONS

1. Propeller blade
2. Scratched or abraded area
3. Crater edge
4. Propeller shaft
5. TRIESTE II structure

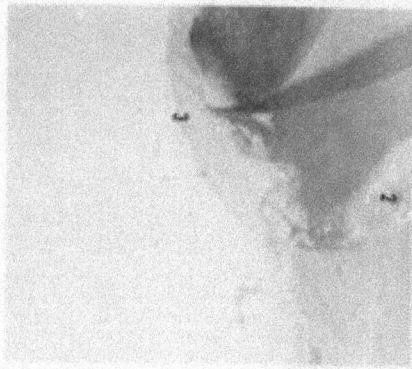

FIG 2

TRIESTE II DIVE 3

FIG 3

MIZAR RUN 79

PLATE X

NAVAL MESSAGE   NAVY DEPARTMENT

INFO COMSTSLANT
NAVOCEANO
COMSTS
NRL
CNO
CINCLANTFLT

OP432

SCORPION - SSN

P 221629Z AUG 68
FM CTU 42.2.1

TO COMSUBLANT

INFO COMSUBRON 8
USNS MIZAR

UNCLAS

SUBJ 8 SRN-9 INSTALLATION/SCORP SEARCH (U).

1. HONEYWELL HX21 COMPUTER BUFFER INSTALLED IN MIZAR BY APL
JOHNS HOPKINS NOT OPERATING PROPERLY WITH SRN-9 SYSTEM AND HAS NOT
OPERATIED PROPERLY SINCE INSTALATION. ERRORS ARE REPORTED TO BE
ASSOCIATED WITH RECEIVING FROM ITT SATELLITE SYSTEM TO SRN-9SYSTEM.
AS PRESENTLY ACCOMPLISHED WITHOUH BUFFER, NAVIGATION REQUIRES MANUAL
INSERTION OF 38 WORDS OF INFO PAREN RE-NAVIGATION MODE NECESSARY
PAREN PLUS NUMEROUS MANUAL RECHECKS FOR SOLUTION ACCURACY.

2. MR BUCHANAN INDICATES THAT THIS PROBLEM HAS BEEN WELL KNOWN BY NRL
AND APL JOHNS HOPKINS AND LONG DISCUSSED BUT NOT CORRECTED DUE TO
LACK OF AGREEMENT AND SUPPORT OF A LONG RANGE PLAN FOR MIZAR SEARCH OPS.
CURRENT INSTALLATION WAS MADE WITH VIEW TO WAR OPS TO ONE AUGUST ONLY.
THIS SITUATION CONTRIBUTING TO NAVPROBS PREVIOUSLY REPORTED BY CAPT
(b)(6)   IN JULY.

3. URGENTLY REQUIRE APL JOHNS HOPKINS DESIGN ENGINEER ON SCENE ASAP TO
CORRECT REWIRING PROBLEM IN BUFFER UNIT IN ORDER TO INCREASE SPEED OF
OUTPUT, DECREASE ERRORS AND MAVFOSITS PD INCREASE ABILITY TO DEFINE
AND RECOVER POSITS QUICKLY AND ACCURATELY.

31 ...COG   00000C
SN ASN(R&D) 00 09 03 32 33 04 43 06 60 07 70 71 75
92 94 JAG NAVSHIPS IP FP BFR SCORPION FILE

M/R: THIS MESSAGE NOT PASSED BY OPNAVCOMMO TO TAG.

PRIORITY
P 031900Z JUN 68
FM COMSUBLANT

TO CINCLANTFLT
COMSECONDFLT
COMNAVAIRLANT
COMSERVLANT
COMASWFORLANT
COMNAVBASE NORVA
COMEASTSEAFRON
COMCRUDESLANT
COMFAIRWINGSLANT
COMINELANT
COMFIVE
COMEASTAREA COAST GUARD

INFO CNO
COMSUBFLOT SIX
SURRONCOMSLANT
COMNAVSHIPSYSCOMHQ
COMSUBFLOT TWO
COMSERVRON EIGHT
USS STANDLEY
COMCRUDESLANTREP NORVA
COMSUBFLOT EIGHT
VCOAC
COMCRUDESFLOT TWO
CTG EIGHT ONE PT FIVE
CTG EIGHT ONE PT NINE

UNCLAS E F T O

3120 SUBMISS SITREP 18

1. SURFACE/SUBMARINE/AIRCRAFT SEARCHS CONTINUING. NO SIGNIFICANT
RESULTS.

2. ANTICIPATE ONE MORE DAY OF SEARCH OPERATIONS BY REQUIN
VICINITY MARSALA BANK AND BY NORWALK VICINITY LAT 28-35N LONG 36-02W.

33(6) ...COG   14420C
SN(5) 00(2) 09(1) 09B(1) 090(1) 90(1) 03(1) 30(3) 31(5) 32(8)
34(2) 04(2) 05(8) 50(16) 51(1) 53(4) 56(3) 06(1) 61(2) 07(1)
75(2) 92(14) 94(12) 95(4) 007(8) IP(5) FP(5) BFR(1) JAG(5)
NATMAP(1) OLA(5) OON(5) PERS(1)   SCORPION-FILE(1) ASNRD(1) + 147

CONTROL NO	PAGE	OF	PAGE	TIME OF RECEIPT	DATE TIME GROUP
C03777/3/HM/F	1		2	03/1938Z	031900Z JUN 68

3. HOIST AND PRESERVER WILL REMAIN AZORES PENDING COMPLETION OF CRUISER BANK AND HYERES BANK SEARCHES.

4. COMPASS ISLAND WILL COMPLETE HER EASTWARD TRANSIT OF SCORPION'S TRACK TO LONG 34W AT ABOUT 032000Z AT WHICH TIME SHE WILL PROCEED DIRECT TO TERCEIRA.

5. NEXT SITREP 040400Z.

MH/CK/B   101314

CALL 53337
FOR NMCC/MC

007...COG
SN 00 09 098 090 90 03 30 31 32 33 34 04 05 50/SERVICE
51 53 56 06 61 07 75 92 94 95 XXXX IP FP BFR
JAG NATMAP OLA OON PERS ASN(R&D) SCORPION

VZCZCJCS017FJC492
PP RUEOJFA
DE RUEDNKA5656 1551948
ZNY EEEEE
P 031910Z JUN 68
FM CINCLANT
TO RUTHBK/COMUSFORAZ
INFO RUEDNKA/CINCLANTFLT
RUEOJFA/OASD(PA)
RUEBAKA/COMSUBLANT
RUEBNFA/COMASWFORLANT
BT
UNCLAS E F T O

RECEIVED AT CNO
COMMUNICATIONS
CENTER

04 00 47 Z JUN 68

5720 RELEASE OF INFORMATION CONCERNING SCORPION SEARCH OPERATIONS
A. COMUSFORAZ 031030Z JUN 68
1. NO OBJECTION TO UTILIZATION OF LOCALLY GENERATED
MATERIAL IN STATION PAPERS OR ON LOCAL NEWS BROADCAST
OF AFRTS OUTLETS PROVIDED THAT THEY DEAL SPECIFICALLY
WITH THE IN-PORT ACTIVITIES OF SEARCH UNITS.
2. NO RELEASES WILL BE MADE CONCERNING AT SEA OPERATIONS
OR ON RESULTS OF AIR SEARCH.
3. IF QUERIED BY LOCAL MEDIA CONCERNING IN-PORT ACTIVITIES
OF SEARCH UNITS, YOU MAY REPLY WITHIN THE FOLLOWING
CONTEXT, AS APPROPRIATE:
'THE SALVAGE SHIPS PRESERVER AND HOIST ARRIVED IN
TERCIERA ON JUNE 2 AND 3 RESPECTIVELY AND COMMENCED
LOADING THE SUBMERSIBLES 'DEEP DIVER' AND THE ADS MARK IV
AND ASSOCIATED EQUIPMENT. THE SOPHISTICATED EQUIPMENT
ABOARD THE TWO SALVAGE SHIPS WILL ONLY BE USED IF THE
SEARCH FOR SCORPION NARROWS TO A SPECIFIC LOCALITY.'
4. THE FOLLOWING COMPOSITE STORY OF SEARCH OPERATIONS TO
THE PRESENT IS FOR INTERNAL MEDIA:
' AT 1:00 P.M. MONDAY, MAY 27, THE NUCLEAR SUBMARINE
SCORPION WAS DUE AT HER HOMEPORT OF NORFOLK, VIRGINIA,
AFTER ROUTINE EXTENDED TRAINING OPERATIONS WITH THE
SIXTH FLEET IN THE MEDITERANNEAN. THE SHIP DEPLOYED FROM
NORFOLK ON FEBRUARY 15. THE LAST OFFICIAL COMMUNICATION
FROM THE SCORPION WAS ON MAY 21, AND WAS A ROUTINE POSITION

INFO: CJCS-1 DJS-3 SJCS-1 J3-8 J5-2 NMCC-1 SAMAA-1 SDEF-7 ASD/ISA-9
ASD/PA-1 DIA-15 CSA-1 CNO-2 CSAF-1 CMC-7 FILE-1(61)TLJ/RD

OF 3

REPORT. IT IS NORMAL FOR SUBMARINES MAKING SUBMERGED
PASSAGE TO MAINTAIN RADIO SILENCE FOR EXTTENDED PERIODS
OF TIME. WHEN THE SCORPION WAS SEVERAL HOURS OVERDUE,
THE ATLANTIC FLEET LAUNCHED A WIDE SEA AND AIR SEARCH
UTILIZING SURFACE SHIPS, SUBMARINES AND LONG RANGE AIR-
CRAFT FROM HOME PORTS ALL ALONG THE EAST COAST AND AIR
BASES IN THE UNITED STATES, BERMUDA, AND THE AZORES.
THE SEARCH FORCES WERE UNDER THE OVERALL COMMAND OF
VICE ADMIRAL ARNOLD F. SCHADE, COMMANDER SUBMARINE
FORCES ATLANTIC FLEET, WITH REAR ADMIRAL LAWRENCE G. BERNARD,
COMMANDER SUBMARINE FLOTILLA SIX, ACTING AS AT SEA COM-
MANDER ABOARD THE GUIDED MISSILE FRIGATE USS STANDLEY.
THE SEARCH FORCE WAS CONTINUALLY AUGMENTED UNTIL, AT ONE
TIME IT NUMBERED 55 SHIPS AND 35 U.S. AND CANADIAN SEARCH
AIRCRAFT DURING THE PEAK PERIOD (28 THROUGH 30 MAY). SEARCH
AIRCRAFT INCLUDED P-2'S, P-3'S, S-2'S AND C-130'S FROM THE NAVY,
AIRFORCE AND COAST GUARD. AS AREAS WERE THOROUGHLY SEARCH-
ED, FORCES WERE REDUCED AND REMAINING SHIPS AND AIRCRAFT
CONCENTRATED THEIR EFFORTS IN OTHER AREAS. ON THE EVENING
OF MAY 29 A BRIEF RADIO MESSAGE WAS PICKED UP BY A
SEARCH PLANE, THE SUBMARINE LAPON, AND SIX SURFACE
SHIPS. THE MESSAGE CONTAINED THE SCORPION'S CODE NAME
'BRANDYWINE'. ALTHOUGH A BEARING WAS OBTAINED ON THE
POSSIBLE AREA FROM WHICH THE MESSAGE COULD HAVE BEEN
SENT SEARCH FORCES AFTER AN EXHAUSTIVE SEARCH WERE UNABLE TO
DETERMINE ITS SOURCE.   THE CODE NAME, HOWEVER,
IS ALSO THE NAME OF SEVERAL CIVILIAN VESSELS IN THE ATLANTIC
AREA, AND IT IS POSSIBLE THAT THE MESSAGE COULD HAVE BEEN
SENT BY ONE OF THEM. INITIALLY THE SEARCH CONCENTRATED
NORTH AND SOUTH ALONG THE CONTINENTAL SHELF OF THE EAST
COAST AT THE WESTERN END OF SCORPION'S PROJECTED TRACK,
AND EASTWARD ALONG THE TRACK TOWARDS SCORPION'S LAST
KNOWN POSITION SOME 360 MILES SOUTH OF THE AZORES. DURING
THE EXTENSIVE SEARCH SEVERAL SMALL OBJECTS SUCH AS BUOYS
AND OIL CANS WERE SIGHTED BY SEARCH UNITS BUT WERE IDENTI-
FIED AS NOT COMING FROM SCORPION. TWO SUNKEN HULKS, ONE
OFF CAPE HENRY, VIRGINIA, AND ONE OFF CAPE CHARLES, WERE
INVESTIGATED BY THE SUBMARINE RESCUE VESSEL SUNBIRD AND

DEPARTMENT OF DEFENSE
NATIONAL MILITARY COMMAND CENTER
MESSAGE CENTER

WERE DETERMINED TO BE WW II SUBMARINE AND THE BARNACLE-
ENCRUSTED HULL OF AN OLD MERCHANT VESSEL. MEANWHILE,
THE SCIENTIFIC RESEARCH SHIP USNS MIZAR LEFT NORFOLK JUNE 2
TO ASSIST SEARCH FORCES OFF THE CRUISER AND IRVING BANKS
SOUTH OF THE AZORES. THE MIZAR IS SCHEDULED TO REACH THE
AREA WITH HER DEEP SEARCH GEAR ON JUNE 9. THE SUBMERSIBLES
DEEP DIVER AND THE ADS MARK IV WERE FLOWN FROM THE UNITED STATES
TO THE AZORES AND ARE BEING LOADED ABOARD THE SALVAGE
VESSELS PRESERVER AND HOIST, TO BE USED IF THE SEARCH
NARROWED TO A SPECIFIC AREA. PRESERVER AND HOIST, WITH
THE EQUIPMENT ABOARD, WILL JOIN THE SEARCH FORCES NEAR
THE CRUISER AND IRVING BANKS. THE FRENCH SUBMARINE
REQUIN JOINED THE SEARCH ON JUNE 2 NEAR THE MARSALA BANK,
400 MILES SOUTHWEST OF THE AZORES AND IS CONTINUING TO
ASSIST U.S. UNITS. ON JUNE 3 A TOTAL OF 22 SHIPS AND 27
ARICRAFT WERE CONTINUING THE SEARCH FOR SCORPION. THE
LARGEST PART OF THIS FORCE IS A GROUP OF SUBMARINES AND
FIVE DESTROYERS WHICH ARE TRANSITING 1600 MILES EASTWARD
FROM NORFOLK ALONG THE SCORPION'S PROJECTED TRACK.
5. YOUR COMMAND WILL BE ADDED TO DISTRIBUTION OF PRESS
UPDATES. INFORMATION CONTAINED THEREIN WILL HAVE BEEN
RELEASED TO THE MEDIA AND MAY BE UTILIZED AS CONSIDERED
APPROPRIATE BY YOU WITH LOCAL MEDIA REPRESENTATIVES.
BT
NNNN

REF A. NOT IDENT

3 OF 3   51591

NAVAL MESSAGE

NAVY DEPARTMENT

```
PRIORITY
P 040608Z JUN 68
FM COMSUBLANT

TO CINCLANTFLT
COMSECONDFLT
COMNAVAIRLANT
COMSERVLANT
COMASWFORLANT
COMNAVBASE NORVA
COMEASTSEAFRON
COMCRUDESLANT
COMFAIRWINGSLANT
COMINELANT
COMFIVE
COMEASTAREA COAST GUARD

INFO CNO
COMSUBFLOT SIX
SUBRONCOMSLANT
COMNAVSHIPSYSCOMHQ
COMSUBFLOT TWO
COMSERVRON EIGHT
USS STANDLEY
COMCRUDESLANTREP NORVA
COMSUBFLOT EIGHT
VCOAC
COMCRUDESFLOT TWO
CTG EIGHT ONE PT FIVE
CTG EIGHT ONE PT NINE
```

UNCLAS E F T O

3120 SUBMISS SITREP 19

1. SURFACE/SUBMARINE SEARCHES CONTINUING. NO SIGNIFICANT RESULTS.

2. 24 VP AIRCRAFT FLIGHTS FLOWN 3 JUN ON OR NEAR SCORPION TRACK. NO SIGHTINGS SUBMARINES ASSOCIATED.

```
33(6) ...COG                                                    14420C
SN(5) 00(2) 09(1) 09B(1) 090(1) 90(1) 03(1) 30(3) 31(5) 32(8)
34(2) 04(2) 05(8) 50(16) 51(1) 53(4) 56(3) 06(1) 61(2) 07(1)
75(2) 92(14) 94(12) 95(4) 007(8) IP(5) FP(5) BFR(1) JAG(5)
NATMAP(1) OLA(5) OON(5) PERS(1) NFOIO SCORPION-FILE(1) ASNRD(1) + 147
```

CONTROL NO	PAGE	OF	PAGE	TIME OF RECEIPT	DATE TIME GROUP
C04901/1/LP/F	1			04/0734Z	040608Z JUN 68

3. NORWALK RECOVERED SEVERAL PLASTIC BOTTLES AND OTHER FLOTSUM
REPORTED BY VP IN VICINITY LAT 28-49N LONG 36-01W. ALL EVALUATED
NON-SUBMARINE ORIGIN.

4. NEXT SITREP 041600Z.

EFTO

NAVAL MESSAGE   NAVY DEPARTMENT
_____

IMMEDIATE
O 041655Z JUN 68
FM CTU FOUR TWO PT TWO PT FOUR

TO TE FOUR TWO PT TWO PT FOUR PT TWO

INFO CNO
CINCLANTFLT
COMSERVLANT
CTG EIGHT ONE PT NINE
CTU FOUR TWO PT TWO PT TWO

UNCLAS E F T O

3120 SUBMISS
CTU 81.9 PASS TO COMSUBLANT REP LAJES
TE 42.2.4.2 PASS TO SUPSALV REP
A. TELECON MY CDR (b)(6) /COMSUBLANT REP LAJES OF 4 JUN 68
B. MY 031557Z JUN 68

1. ON COMPLETION FUELING PONTA DELGADA PRESERVER GET UNDERWAY AND
PROCEED VICINITY LAT 31-55N LONG 28-00W TO CONDUCT EXPLORATORY
SEARCH ON TOP OF CRUISER BANK PLATEAU WITH DEEP DIVER. ADVISE IF
NAV REFERENCE WILL BE REQUIRED.

2. UTILIZE OBSS FOR SEARCH AT DISCRETION OF COMMANDING OFFICER
UTILIZING TECHNICAL ADVICE OF PERSONNEL ON BOARD.

3. FOR SUPSALV REP, DESIGNATE TECHNICAL ADVISOR IN CHARGE.

4. ANTICIPATE DURATION OF OPS ON CRUISER BANK TWO DIVING DAYS.
SUBMIT TWELVE HOUR SITREPS AT 0000Z AND 1200Z. FILE OWN UNCLAS MOVREP.

33(6) ...COG   14420C
SN(5) 00(2) 09(1) 09B(1) 09D(1) 90(1) 03(1) 30(3) 31(5) 32(8)
34(2) 04(2) 05(8) 50(16) 51(1) 53(4) 56(3) 06(1) 61(2) 07(1)
75(2) 92(14) 94(12) 95(4) 007(8) IP(5) FP(5) BFR(1) JAG(5)
NATMAP(1) OLA(5) OON(5) PERS(1) NFOIO SCORPION-FILE(1) ASNRD(1) +
NAVSHIPS   147

CONTROL NO	PAGE	OF	PAGE	TIME OF RECEIPT	DATE TIME GROUP
C05506/4/NF/	1		1	04/1736Z	041655Z JUN 68

PRIORITY
P 031548Z JUN 68
FM COMSUBLANT

TO FRENCH SUBMARINE REQUIN

INFO ALSOUMAR
CNO
CINCLANTFLT
TG FOUR TWO PT TWO

UNCLAS

A. COMSUBLANT 011656Z JUN 68

1. YOUR THOROUGH SEARCH OF AREA AND TIMELY REPORTING IS MOST VALUABLE
TO OUR SEARCH EFFORT. WITH YOUR EFFORT, SEARCH OF ENTIRE AREA
ALONG TRACK IS NOW UNDERWAY.

2. UNLESS SIGNIFICANT INFORMATION OBTAINED DESIRE YOU CONTINUE SEARCH
REQUESTED REF A UNTIL 041200Z. AT THAT TIME, IN ORDER TO AVOID INTER-
FERENCE WITH OTHER UNITS OF SEARCH FORCE, REQUEST YOU REMAIN ON SURFACE
UNTIL NORTH OF LAT 40N WHILE DEPARTING AREA.

3. UPON YOU DEPARTURE REQUEST FINAL SITREP INCLUDING YOUR INTENDED
MOVEMENTS.

83(6) ...COG   144200
SN(5) 00(2) 09(1) 09B(1) 090(1) 90(1) 03(1) 30(3) 31(5) 32(8)
84(2) 04(2) 05(8) 50(16) 51(1) 53(4) 56(3) 06(1) 61(2) 07(1)
95(2) 92(14) 94(12) 95(4) 007(8) IP(5) FP(5) BFR(1) JAG(5)
NATMAP(1) OLA(5) OON(5) PERS(1) NFOIO SCORPION-FILE(1) ASNRD(1) +
NAVSHIPS   147

CORR PER SVC 032567/6/GS	PAGE 1	PAGE 1	TIME OF RECEIPT 03/1713Z	DATE TIME GROUP 031548Z JUN 68
C03476/2/JB/				

NAVAL MESSAGE   NAVY DEPARTMENT

PRIORITY
P 040405Z JUN 68
FM SS REQUIN

TO RUEBAKA/COMSUBLANT

INFO CNO
CINCLANTFLT
MMFSACLANT

UNCLAS

MY POSITION 3352N 3417W AT 040400Z CONDUCTED SURFACE SURVEY
NORTH EAST PAR OF E AREA SOUNDINGS DEEPER THAN 2900 METERS
I INND TO DIVE THIS POSITION UNTIL 040587 FOR ACOUSTIC
RESEARCH THAN LEAVE THE AREA 041200Z

THIS MESSAGE RECEIVED GARBLED. WILL
OBTAIN CORRECTED COPY UPON REQUEST

33(6) ...COG   14420C
SN(5) 00(2) 09(1) 09B(1) 090(1) 90(1) 03(1) 30(3) 31(5) 32(8)
34(2) 04(2) 05(8) 50(16) 51(1) 53(4) 56(3) 06(1) 61(2) 07(1)
75(2) 92(14) 94(12) 95(4) 007(8) IP(5) FP(5) BFR(1) JAG(5)
NATHAP(1) OLA(5) OON(5) PERS(1) NFOIO SCORPION-FILE(1) ASNRD(1) +
NAVSHIPS   147

	PAGE	OF	PAGE	TIME OF RECEIPT	DATE TIME GROUP
C04837/1/LP/F	1		1	04/0642Z	040405Z JUN

NAVAL MESSAGE NAVY DEPARTMENT

ROUTINE
R 032033Z JUN 68
FM NAVSUPSYSCOMHQ

TO COMAC (MACTRAR) SCOTT AFB

INFO NAVSHIPSYSCOMHQ
NSC NORFOLK
NAF LAJES
NAVAIRSYSCOMHQ
NAVTRANSCO NORFOLK
COMSUBLANT
CNO
JCS
HQUSAF
21AF MCGUIRE AFB
22AF TRAVIS AFB

UNCLAS

CNO (OP404) JCS(J4B) HQUSAF(AFSTP).
REQUEST FOR SPECIAL ASSIGNMENT AIRLIFT (SCORPION SUBMISS)
A. FONECON CAPT (b)(6) /COMAC MR. TRUSSELL/NAVSUP OF 1 JUNE
B. FONECON LCDR (b)(6) /NSC NORFOLK MR. TRUSSELL/NAVSUP OF 1 JUNE

1. CFM REF (A) AND IAW RQMNTS SUBMITTED BY REF (B) REQUEST PRIORITY
S1-A(1) SPECIAL ASSIGNMENT AIRLIFT OPERATE NAS NORFOLK/LAJES,
AZORES. SAAM NBR 2000 ASSIGNED. TAC N248. MATL AVBL 2 JUNE. REQ DEL
2 JUNE.

2. RQMNTS CONSIST 41 PCS SONAR BUOYS AND EQUIPMENT. WGT 51,735 LBS
CUBE 2173. DMN. WGT LSI 48L X 40W X 47H: 1262 LBS.

3. ORIGION CONTACT: MR. ABBOTT NTCO NORFOLK AUTOVON (b)(6)
DSTN CONTACT. CDR (b)(6) COMSUBLANT LAJES, AZORES

4. REQ FOLLOWING BE INCL ON FLT ADVY: NSC NORFOLK, CNO, NAVAIRSYSCOMHQ
NAF LAJES, NAVTANSCO NORFOLK, NAVSUPSYSCOMHQ (052)

HD ...COG 14420C
SN(5) 00(2) 09(1) 09B(1) 090(1) 90(1) 03(1) 30(3) 31(5) 32(8)
34(2) 04(2) 05(8) 50(16) 51(1) 53(4) 56(3) 06(1) 61(2) 07(1)
75(2) 92(14) 94(12) 95(4) 007(8) IP(5) FP(5) BFR(1) JAG(5)
NATNAP(1) OLA(5) OON(5) PERS(1) NFOIO SCORPION-FILE(1) ASNRD(1)

CONTROL NO	PAGE	OF	PAGE	TIME OF RECEIPT	DATE TIME GROUP
C04624/1/LP/F	1		1	04/0353Z	032033Z JUN 68

PRIORITY
P 031715Z JUN 68
FM SS REQUIN

TO COMSUBLANT

INFO CNO
CINCLANTFLT
HMFSACLANT

UNCLAS

MY POSITION 031600Z 3341N 3450N STOP CONDUCTED SURVEY
AND SURFACE SEARCH IN WESTERN PART OF AREA STOP ALL
SOUNDINGS GREATER THAN 2900 METRES EXCEPT 2000 METRES
VICINITY 3343N 3501W STOP FOUND SEVERAL FISHING NETS
FLOATERS SOME OF THEM COLOURED IN INTERNATIONAL ORANGE
STOP U. S. S. COMPASS ISLAND SURVEYING IN VICINITY
STOP WE ARE KEEPING U. S. F. CONTACT STOP INTEND TO SURVEY
NORTHEAST PART OF THE AREA AND IF NO OTHER CLUE LEAVE
THE AREA IN DIRECTION OF PUNTA DELGADA AT 041000Z

33(6) ...COG   144200
SN(5) 00(2) 09(1) 098(1) 090(1) 90(1) 03(1) 30(3) 31(5) 32(8)
34(2) 04(2) 05(8) 50(16) 51(1) 53(4) 56(3) 06(1) 61(2) 07(1)
75(2) 92(14) 94(12) 95(4) 007(8) IP(5) FP(5) BFR(1) JAG(5)
NATMAP(1) OLA(5) OON(5) PERS(1) NFOIO SCORPION-FILE(1) ASNRD(1) *
                                                                        147

ORIGINATORS NO	PAGE	OF	PAGE	TIME OF RECEIPT	DATE TIME GROUP
C04405/1/HM/F	1		1	04/0159Z	031715Z JUN 68

NAVAL MESSAGE   NAVY DEPARTMENT

IMMEDIATE
O 040444Z JUN 68
FM COMASWFORLANT

TO CINCLANTFLT

INFO CNO
COMSUBLANT
CONFAIRWINGSLANT
CTU FOUR TWO PT TWO PT ONE
CTG EIGHT ONE PT TWO
CTG EIGHT ONE PT THREE
CTG EIGHT ONE PT FOUR
CTG EIGHT ONE PT FIVE
CTG EIGHT ONE PT NINE

UNLAS E F T O

5120 SCORPION SAR AIR SURVEILLANCE SITREP SIX

1. SUMMARY OF ALL FLIGHTS 03 JUNE AS FOLLOWS:
(ALFA) AZORES: FIVE P3 FLIGHTS DURING DAYLIGHT HOURS. NORWALK VECTORED
TO VICINITY 28-49N 36-01W ARRIVED APPROX 031200Z AND RECOVERED VARIOUS
OBJECTS, IDENTIFIED AS FLARE CASE, SIX FOOT FLORESCENT LIGHTS AND FISHING
NET FLOAT. LATER NORWALK RECOVERED LARGE PLASTIC BOTTLES AND SEVERAL THIN
PLASTIC PERFORATED SHEET MATERIAL ABOUT TWO BY TWO INCHES SQUARE. MATERIAL
EVALUATED AS NON-SUBMARINE ASSOCIATED. SECOND FLIGHT LOCATED FADED
ORANGE BALLOON AT 30-15N 31-34W. FINAL FLIGHT SIGHTED ORANGE OBJECT
AT 27-00N 35-55W. OBJECT APPEARED TO BE AFLOAT OR RUBBER BALL. NO
OTHER SIGINIFICANT CONTACTS.
(BRAVER) BERMUDA: SEVEN FLIGHTS (FOUR P3, TWO USAF C-130 AND ONE
USCG C-130) FLOWN. SECOND P3 FLIGHT TO AREA C-2 REPORTED SIGHTING
STANDARD BRIGHT ORANGE LIFE RING WITH FOUR BLACK MARKS SPACED 90
DEGREES APART AND STANDARD LIFE LINE ATTACHED TO OUTER CIRCUMFERENCE
AT 031740Z POSIT 38-50N 54-40Z. SAME FLIGHT REPORTED
DETECTING SPOSSIBLE EXPLOSIONS AT 2115Z ON 2 SONOBUOYS
POSIT 38-13N 55-22W AND 38-08N 54-33W. SOUND REACHED EASTERN BUOY
TEN SECONDS PRIOR TO SECOND BUOY. SPACING ABOUT TWO MINUTES BETWEEN
EXPLOSIONS. EVALUATED AS ORIGINATING FROM ARCTIC SEAL VICINITY 42N 52W.
NO OTHER SIGINICANT CONTACTS.
(CHARLIE) NORVA: TOTAL OF TWELVE P3 AND P2 FLIGHTS, NOTHING
SIGNIFICANT LOCATED.

33(6) ...COG   14420C
SN(5) 00(2) 09(1) 05B(1) 090(1) 9D(1) 03(1) 30(3) 31(5) 32(8)
34(2) 04(2) 05(8) 50(16) 51(1) 53(4) 56(3) 06(1) 61(2) 07(1)
75(2) 92(14) 94(12) 95(4) 007(8) IP(5) FP(5) BFR(1) JAG(5)
NATMAP(1) OLA(5) OON(5) PERS(1) NFOIO SCORPION-FILE(1) ASNRD(1) +
NAVSHIPS   147

NAVAL MESSAGE   NAVY DEPARTMENT

IMMEDIATE
O 031555Z JUN 68
FM CTU FOUR PT TWO PT FOUR

TO CTE FOUR TWO PT TWO PT FOUR PT TWO
CTE FOUR TWO PT TWO PT FOUR PT FIVE

INFO TG FOUR TWO PT TWO
CINCLANTFLT
CNO
COMSERVLANT
CTG EIGHT ONE PT NINE

UNCLAS E F T O

3120 SUBMISS
CTG 81.9 PASS TO COMSUBLANT REP

1. IN VIEW OF GATO SEARCH RESULTS INDICATING LOW PROBABILITY
OF BOTTOMED SUBMARINE VICINITY CRUISER SEA MOUNT AND LACK OF ACCURATE
BATHYMETRIC DATA FOR THAT AREA;
A. HOIST ON COMPLETION EUQIPMENT INSTALLATION AND LOADING REMAIN
BAHIA PRAIA, TERCEIRA,
B. PRESERVER ON COMPLETION EQUIPMENT INSTALLATION AND LOADING
PROCEED PUNTA DELGADA FOR DIESEL FUELING,

2. FURTHER INSTRUCTIONS WILL BE ISSUED DIRECTING MOVEMENTS OF HOIST
AND PRESERVER FROM ABOVE PORTS,

M/R THIS MSG PASSED TO NAVSHIPSSYSCOMHQ BY OPNAVCOMMO.

33(6) ...COG   14420C
SN(5) 00(2) 09(1) 09B(1) 090(1) 90(1) 03(1) 30(3) 31(5) 32(8)
34(2) 04(2) 05(8) 50(16) 51(1) 53(4) 56(3) 06(1) 61(2) 07(1)
75(2) 92(14) 94(12) 95(4) 007(8) IP(5) FP(5) BFR(1) JAG(5)
NATMAP(1) OLA(5) OON(5) PERS(1) NFOIO SCORPION-FILE(1) ASNRD(1) + 147

CONTROL NO	PAGE	OF	PAGE	TIME OF RECEIPT	DATE TIME GROUP
C04351/3/HM/F	1		1	04/0036Z	031555Z JUN 68

NAVAL MESSAGE

NAVY DEPARTMENT

IMMEDIATE
O 032007Z JUN 68
FM CTG FOUR TWO PT TWO

TO TE FOUR TWO PT TWO PT FOUR PT THREE

INFO CTU FOUR TWO PT TWO PT ONE
CINCLANTFLT
TE FOUR TWO PT TWO PT FOUR PT SIX
CNO
CTG EIGHT ONE PT NINE
COMASWFORLANT

EFTO

UNCLAS E F T O

3120 SUBMISS
A. CTG 42.2 022123Z JUN 68

1. TE 42.2.4.6 PROCEEDING NEW SEARCH AREA IN ACCORDANCE PARA
(1) REF A.

2. PROCEED VICINITY LAT 31-30N 29-00W AND OPERATE IN ACCORDANCE
WITH INSTRUCTIONS CTE 42.2.4.6

M/R THIS MSG PASSED TO NAVSHIPSYSCOMHQ BY OPNRVCOMMO

33(6) ...COG   14420C
SN(5) 00(2) 09(1) 09B(1) 090(1) 90(1) 03(1) 30(3) 31(5) 32(8)
34(2) 04(2) 05(8) 50(16) 51(1) 53(4) 56(3) 06(1) 61(2) 07(1)
75(2) 92(14) 94(12) 95(4) 007(8) IP(5) FP(5) BFR(1) JAG(5)
NATMAP(1) OLA(5) OON(5) PERS(1) NFOIO SCORPION-FILE(1) ASNRD(1) + 147

CONTROL NO		PAGE	OF	PAGE	TIME OF RECEIPT	DATE TIME GROUP
C04297/3/HM/		1		1	03/2020Z	032007Z JUN 68

NAVAL MESSAGE   NAVY DEPARTMENT

ROUTINE
R 032048Z JUN 68
FM NAVOCEANO

TO OCEANAV

INFO NRL
COMSUBLANT
USNS MIZAR
APPLIED PHYSICS LAB JOHNS HOPKINS UNIVERSITY
CNO
COMASWFORLANT
USNUSL NLON

UNCLAS

3120 SCORPION SUBMISS SUPPORT
A. YOUR 312115Z MAY 68 .
B. MY 312137Z MAY 68 NOTAL
C. USN/USL 011416Z JUN 68 NOTAL

1. IAW REF A NAVOCEANO SUPPLIED THE FOLLOWING EQUIPMENT AND
PERSONNEL:
A. ONE SRN-9 NAV SYSTEM IN COORDINATION WITH APL.
B. TWO LC-400 LORAN CHARLIE SYSTEMS.
C. AUX EQUIPMENT AS REQUESTED BY NRL CODE 7130.
D. ONE CARTOGRAPHER WITH PHOTOGRAMMETRY BACKGROUND AS PER REF B.
E. NECESSARY PERSONNEL TO INSTALL/MAINTAIN AND OPERATE ABOVE
EQUIPMENT.
F. ONE LORAN C RCVR SHIPPED FM USN/USL PER REF C.

M/R THIS MSG PASSED TO NAVSHIPSSYSCOMHQ BY OPNAVCOMMO.

33(6) ...COG   14420C
SN(5) 00(2) 09(1) 09B(1) 090(1) 90(1) 03(1) 30(3) 31(5) 32(8)
34(2) 04(2) 05(8) 50(16) 51(1) 53(4) 56(3) 06(1) 61(2) 07(1)
75(2) 92(14) 94(12) 95(4) 007(8) IP(5) FP(5) BFR(1) JAG(5)
NATMAP(1) OLA(5) OON(5) PERS(1) NFOIO SCORPION-FILE(1) ASNRD(1) + 147

CONTROL NO	PAGE	OF	PAGE	TIME OF RECEIPT	DATE TIME GROUP
C04350/3/HM/F	1		1	04/0038Z	032048Z JUN 68

NAVAL MESSAGE

NAVY DEPARTMENT

ROUTINE
R 051148Z JUN 68
FM CINCLANTFLT

TO USS PURDY
USS SOLEY

INFO CNO
COMSUBLANT
COMCRUDESFLOT
COMCRUDESFLOT TWO
COMNAVRESTRACOMD
LANTREPNAVRESTRACOM
COMRESDESRON THREE ZERO
COMRESDESRON THREE FOUR

UNCLAS E F T O

3130 SCORPION SAR

1. YOUR PROMPT AND GALLANT RESPONSE UNDER ADVERSE CONDITIONS TO THE
INITIAL EMERGENCY OF THE SCORPION SUBMISS IS NOTED WIH PRIDE AND
PLEASURE. WELL DONE.

EFTO

33(6) ...COG   14420C
SN(5) 00(2) 09(1) 09B(1) 090(1) 90(1) 03(1) 30(3) 31(5) 32(6)
34(2) 04(2) 05(8) 50(16) 51(1) 53(4) 56(3) 06(1) 61(2) 07(1)
 5(2) 92(14) 94(12) 95(4) 007(8) IP(5) FP(5) BFR(1) JAG(5)
MATMAP(1) OLA(5) OON(5) PERS(1)   SCORPION-FILE(1) ASNRD(1) + 147

CONTROL NO	PAGE	OF	PAGE	TIME OF RECEIPT	DATE TIME GROUP
CO7260/4/MV/	1		1	05/1602Z	0511 Z JUN 68

IMMEDIATE
O 040444Z JUN 68
FM COMASWFORLANT

4 JUNE 10 07 2

TO CINCLANTFLT

INFO CNO
COMSUBLANT
COMFAIRWINGSLANT
CTU FOUR TWO PT TWO PT ONE
CTG EIGHT ONE PT TWO
CTG EIGHT ONE PT THREE
CTG EIGHT ONE PT FOUR
CTG EIGHT ONE PT FIVE
CTG EIGHT ONE PT NINE

FILE COPY

THIS IS A CORRECTED COPY
PLEASE DESTROY PREVIOUS COPIES

UNLAS E F T O

3120 SCORPION SAR AIR SURVEILLANCE SITREP SEVEN

1. SUMMARY OF ALL FLIGHTS 03 JUNE AS FOLLOWS:
(ALFA) AZORES: FIVE P3 FLIGHTS DURING DAYLIGHT HOURS. NORWALK VECTORED
TO VICINITY 28-40N 36-01W ARRIVED APPROX 031200Z AND RECOVERED VARIOUS
OBJECTS, IDENTIFIED AS FLARE CASE, SIX FOOT FLORESCENT LIGHTS AND FISHING
NET FLOAT. LATER NORWALK RECOVERED LARGE PLASTIC BOTTLES AND SEVERAL THIN
PLASTIC PERFORATED SHEET MATERIAL ABOUT TWO BY TWO INCHES SQUARE. MATERIAL
EVALUATED AS NON-SUBMARINE ASSOCIATED. SECOND FLIGHT LOCATED FADED
ORANGE BALLOON AT 30-15N 31-34W. FINAL FLIGHT SIGHTED ORANGE OBJECT
AT 27-00N 35-55W. OBJECT APPEARED TO BE AFLOAT OR RUBBER BALL. NO
OTHER SIGINIFICANT CONTACTS.
(BRAVER) BERMUDA: SEVEN FLIGHTS (FOUR P3, TWO USAF C-130 AND ONE
USCG C-130) FLOWN. SECOND P3 FLIGHT TO AREA C-2 REPORTED SIGHTING
STANDARD BRIGHT ORANGE LIFE RING WITH FOUR BLACK MARKS SPACED 90
DEGREES APART AND STANDARD LIFE LINE ATTACHED TO OUTER CIRCUMFERENCE
AT 031740Z POSIT 38-50N 54-40Z. SAME FLIGHT REPORTED
DETECTING SPOSSIBLE EXPLOSIONS AT 2115Z ON 2 SONOBUOYS
POSIT 38-13N 55-22W AND 38-08N 54-33W. SOUND REACHED EASTERN BUOY
TEN SECONDS PRIOR TO SECOND BUOY. SPACING ABOUT TWO MINUTES BETWEEN
EXPLOSIONS. EVALUATED AS ORIGINATING FROM ARCTIC SEAL VICINITY 42N 52W.
NO OTHER SIGNINICANT CONTACTS.
(CHARLIE) NORVA: TOTAL OF TWELVE P3 AND P2 FLIGHTS. NOTHING

SIGNIFICANT LOCATED.

33(6) ...COG   144280
SN(5) 00(2) 09(1) 09B(1) 090(1) 90(1) 03(1) 30(3) 31(5) 32(8)
34(2) 04(2) 05(8) 50(16) 51(1) 53(4) 56(3) 06(1) 61(2) 07(1)
75(2) 92(14) 94(12) 95(4) 007(8) IP(5) FP(5) BFR(1) JAG(5)
NATNAP(1) OLA(5) OQN(5) PERS(1) NFOIO SCORPION-FILE(1) ASNRD(1) +
NAVSHIPS   CORR PER   0812Z SVC/BE/5//   147

	PAGE	OF	PAGE	TIME OF RECEIPT	DATE TIME GROUP
004865/I/LP/F	1			04/0545Z	040444Z JUN 68

NAVAL MESSAGE

NAVY DEPARTMENT

```
IMMEDIATE
O 051930Z JUN 68
FM COMSUBLANT

TO COMSTSLANT
CTG EIGHT ONE PT NINE

INFO CINCLANTFLT
CTU FOUR TWO PT TWO PT ONE
DIRSPECPROJ
PMOLANT
POMFLANT
NAVORDSYSCOMHQ
NAVSUPSYSCOMHQ
COMASWFORLANT
CNO
```

EFTO

UNCLAS E F T O

3120 SUBMISS
CTG 81.9 PASS TO COMSUBLANT REP LAJES
A. COMASWFORLANT 051718Z JUN 68 (NOTAL)

1. FOR COMSTSLANT, REQUEST DIRECT NORWALK PROCEED LAT 30-53N
LONG 37-53W TO SEARCH AREA FOR A BRIGHT ORANGE BASKETBALL SIZE
SPHERE SIGHTED BY AIRCRAFT OF TG 81.9.

2. FOR COMSUBLANT REP, REQUEST EVALUATION OF PHOTOGRAPHS TAKEN BY
AIRCRAFT.

3. REF A ADVISES THAT AIRCRAFT WILL SEARCH AREA AT FIRST LIGHT
6 JUNE.

35 copies

M/R THIS MSG PASSED TO NFOIO NAVHIPS BY OPNAVCOMMO
```
33(6) ...COG                                                    14420C
SN(5) 00(2) 09(1) 09B(1) 090(1) 90(1) 03(1) 30(3) 31(5) 32(8)
34(2) 04(2) 05(8) 50(16) 51(1) 53(4) 56(3) 06(1) 61(2) 07(1)
75(2) 92(14) 94(12) 95(4) 007(8) IP(5) FP(5) BFR(1) JAG(5)
NATMAP(1) OLA(5) OON(5) PERS(1) NFOIO SCORPION-FILE(1) ASNRD(1) ↓ 147
```

CONTROL NO	PAGE	OF	PAGE	TIME OF RECEIPT	DATE TIME GROUP
C07655/3/BC/F	1		1	05/1956Z	051930Z JUN 68

NAVAL MESSAGE

NAVY DEPARTMENT

PRIORITY
P 050505Z JUN 68
FM COMSUBLANT

TO CINCLANTFLT
COMSECONDFLT
COMNAVAIRLANT
COMSERVLANT
COMASWFORLANT
COMNAVBASE NORVA
COMEASTSEAFRON
COMCRUDESLANT
COMFAIRWINGSLANT
COMINELANT
COMFIVE
COMEASTAREA COAST GUARD

INFO CNO
COMSUBFLOT SIX
SURRONCOMSLANT
COMNAVSHIPSYSCOMHQ
COMSUBFLOT TWO
COMSERVRON EIGHT
USS STANDLEY
COMCRUDESLANTREP NORVA
COMSUBFLOT EIGHT
VCOAC
COMCRUDESFLOT TWO
CTG 81.5
CTG 81.9

UNCLAS E F T O

3120 SUBMISS SITREP 21

1. SURFACE SEARCH UNIT AT 31-39N, 32-55W; SUBMARINE SEARCH UNIT AT
33-23N, 36-17W CONTINUING SEARCH ENROUTE LAST KNOW POSIT.

2. GATO/KITTIWAKE CONTINUING INVESTIGATION HYERES BANK.

3. NORWALK AT 040900Z AT POSIT 28-42N, 35-57W RECOVERED FLOTSAM

33(6) ...COG   144203
SN(5) 00(2) 09(1) 09B(1) 090(1) 90(1) 03(1) 30(3) 31(5) 32(8)
34(2) 04(2) 05(8) 50(16) 51(1) 53(4) 56(3) 06(1) 61(2) 07(1)
75(2) 92(14) 94(12) 95(4) 007(8) IP(5) FP(5) BFR(1) JAG(5)
NATMAP(1) OLA(5) OON(5) PERS(1) NFOIO SCORPION-FILE(1) ASNRD(1)

NO	PAGE	OF	PAGE	TIME OF RECEIPT	DATE TIME GROUP
C06691/1/DB/F	1		2	05/0632Z	050505Z JUN 68

DESCRIBED AS QUOTE SOFT RUBBER PIPE COVERING FOUR INCH DIA BY
EIGHTEEN INCHES LONG. SEVERAL LAYERS OF PAINT INDICATE IT HAS BEEN
PAINTED GRAY GREEN GRAY. PAINT IS SOFT AND BLISTERED. UNABLE TO
DETERMINE IF FROM FIRE OR LONG EXPOSURE IN WATER. NO RADIATION.
UNQUOTE.

4. SUNBIRD DIVER IDENTIFIED PARGO UNCHARTED OBJECT AT 37-12.1N,
74-45.3W AS LARGE SUNKEN BARGE IN 224 FEET OF WATER.

5. FRENCH SUBMARINE REQUIN COMPLETED SEARCH MARSALA BANK. DEPARTED
ON SURFACE FOR PONTA DELGADA AT 041200Z. ETA 060900Z.

EFTO

NAVAL MESSAGE

IMMEDIATE
O 061650Z JUN 68
FM CTG FOUR TWO PT TWO

TO CTE FOUR TWO PT TWO PT FOUR PT FIVE
CTE FOUR TWO PT TWO PT FOUR PT TWO

INFO CNO
CNM
CINCLANTFLT
CINCUSNAVEUR
DSSP (PM II)
COMSERVLANT
COMSERVRON EIGHT
CTG EIGHT ONE
CTG EIGHT ONE PT NINE
EXP DIVING UNIT
COMSECONDFLT
CTU FOUR TWO PT TWO PT ONE

UNCLAS E F T O

3120 SCORPION SUBMISS
CTG 81.9 PASS TO COMSUBLANT REP LAJES
CTF 42.2.4.2 PASS TO SUPSALVREP

1. SEARCH OPERATIONS INVOLVING HOIST AND PRESERVER HAVE BEEN TERMINATED.
FOLLOWING INSTRUCTIONS APPLY:
   A. FOR PRESERVER, DEPART PUNTA DELGADA AND PROCEED BAHIA PRAIA.
UPON ARRIVAL OFFLOAD DEEP DIVER, OBSS, AND ASSOCIATED EQUIPMENT.
   B. FOR HOIST: RETURN CONUS WITH ADS-4 AND ASSOCIATED EQUIPMENT
ON HOIST INCLUDING AIR SALVAGE HOSE SUPPLIED TO BOTH HOIST AND PRESERVER.
   C. FOR SUPSALVREP LCDR (b) (6)   . REQUEST YOU ARRANGE FOR AIRLIFT
OF DEEP DIVER AND ASSOCIATED EQUIPMENT TO CONUS. FURTHER REQUEST YOU
DESIGNATE TWO PERSONNEL TO ACCOMPANY ADS-4 ON HOIST. ONE OF TWO PERSONNEL
ASSIGNED IS TO BE A REPRESENTATIVE OF OCEAN SYSTEM INC.

2. REQUEST COMSECONDFLT PROVIDE ONWARD ROUTING INSTRUCTIONS TO HOIST AND
PRESERVER.

33(6) ...COG   14420C
SN(5) 00(2) 09(1) 09B(1) 090(1) 90(1) 03(1) 30(3) 31(5) 32(8)
34(2) 04(2) 05(8) 50(16) 51(1) 53(4) 56(3) 06(1) 61(2) 07(1)
70(2) 92(14) 94(12) 95(4) 007(8) IP(5) FP(5) BFR(1) JAG(5)
NATMAP(1) OLA(5) OON(5) PERS(1) NFOIO SCORPION-FILE(1) ASNRD(1) + 147
NAVSHIPS

CONTROL NO	PAGE	OF	PAGE	TIME OF RECEIPT	DATE TIME GROUP
C09367/2/MH/F	1		1	06/1728Z	061650Z JUN 68

NEWS FROM
U. S. NAVY
MILITARY SEA TRANSPORTATION SERVICE
ATLANTIC HEADQUARTERS
PUBLIC AFFAIRS OFFICE
58TH STREET AND FIRST AVENUE
BROOKLYN, NEW YORK 11250

VERRAZANO-NARROWS BRIDGE, GATEWAY TO HEADQUARTERS, MILITARY SEA TRANSPORTATION SERVICE, ATLANTIC

cable address: COMSTSLANT

telephone: 212 — GEdney 9-5400, ext. 5108/5109

U. S. Government Autovon: 488-5108/5109

31 October 1968

FOR RELEASE ONLY BY CHIEF OF INFORMATION, U.S. NAVY

(ATLANTIC HEADQUARTERS, MILITARY SEA TRANSPORTATION SERVICE, U.S. NAVY, BROOKLYN, N.Y.) -- JO1 SAM HERZOG, Navy Journalist in the Public Affairs Office of the Atlantic Commander, Military Sea Transportation Service (COMSTSLANT), rode the U.S. Naval Ship MIZAR (T-AGOR-11) during the initial two weeks of her search for the nuclear powered submarine SCORPION (31 May - 13 June 1968). Following is Journalist Herzog's account of the beginning of the search for SCORPION:

THE MIZAR GOES ON A HUNT

By JO1 Sam Herzog

What would you want if you were given the job of looking for a brooken needle in a four square mile haystack from a helicopter? Having a good helicopter, acurate navigation, a magnet and a camera would be some of the most desirable tools for a search like that.

A similar problem faced the USNS MIZAR (T-AGOR-11) as it searched the mid-Atlantic for the missing submarine SCORPION, and the ship had the tools for the job.

The MIZAR scurried out of the Norfolk Naval Base on Sunday, June 2 under orders from the Commander-in-Chief of the Navy's Atlantic Fleet to join in the search. The ship, with its Master, Captain James D.

-more-

7

Hobbs, its officers and crew, and the scientific team, with its Senior
Scientist, Dr. Chester L. Buchanan, and his team members, are performing
a key function in the continuing search for the remains of the lost
nuclear submarine.

The MIZAR's pecular qualities and spaces, coupled with the scientific
equipment and instruments, make the ship unusually well qualified for
this particular type of hunt. In 1964 the MIZAR was the first ship to
locate and photograph the remains of the USS THRESHER in 8,400 feet of
water off the Massachusetts coast. The MIZAR team also played a key role
in the search for the lost nuclear device off Palomaris, Spain, in April,
1966.

Designated an oceanographic research ship (T-AGOR), the MIZAR started
its MSTSLANT career as a polar supply ship with an icebreaker type bow
and a cruiser type stern and ice station controls mounted in a tower
near the bow. Outwardly she has changed little. The cargo booms amidships have been replaced by a large trapazoidial "house" ca-led the
wellhouse. However, internally many changes have been made. There is
now a large "hole" in the bottom of the MIZAR, extending from her main
deck down through her hull. The "house" covers this "hole" which is
then covered at deck level by two hydralically operated doors. The carro
hold now contains large reels of heavy cable and line instead of the
Arctic supplies it once carried. Other cargo spaces have been converted
into quarters for the scientists- a photo lab, an electronics lab, an
electronics technician's shop, a navigational aids room and a control
center. Completely air-conditioned, the spaces are never empty as the
scientists work in two teams, each team working 12 to 14 hours a day.

-more-

7

Designated BLUE and GOLD as are the Navy's Polaris submarine crews,
the work day is divided logically along the meal-time hours. On this
particular mission, the BLUE team, headed by Senior Scientist Buchanan,
works from midnight to 7 a.m. and from noon to 5 p.m. The GOLD team,
headed by Research Physicist(Electro-Acoustical) Robert B. Patterson,
works the other 12 hours. Both these men are Naval Research Laboratory
employees(NRL) as are nine more of the scientists. The Naval Oceanographic Office(NAVOCEANO) provided the other four scientists who round
out the 13 man scientific team. Along with Captain Hobbs and his 40-man
crew, they comprise the MIZAR team which left Pier #2 in Norfolk, Virginia, on Sunday morning, June 2, to search for the SCORPION.

This was not in any sense a routine voyage and consequently there was
more than the usual amount of rush and confusion to get the ship loaded
with stores and equipment and get it out to sea. Added to that was the
fact that the ship had only pulled into Norfolk on Wednesday, expecting
a yard period and most of the scientific gear had been removed for
further test and evaluation.

Crewmen like Robert Leonhardt of Babalon, Long Island, an Ordinary
Seaman who had to cancel his plans to go home on leave and see his oldest
son, an Air Force Sergeant, who was coming home on leave from Vietnam,
were effected as well as scientists like Physicist Robert B. Patterson
who had just finished a cruise on the MIZAR and was looking forward to
some time at home with his family in Washington, D.C.

But the attitude of all concerned was one of dedication. As the First
Officer, Mr. Sixto Mangual of New Bedford, Mass., said, "When I told my
family we are going out to try and find the SCORPION, my son says to me,
"you hurry up and find them and bring them home!" But Senior Scientist

-more-

7

"Buck" Buchanan was not as optimistic. As he briefed the scientific

team with the ship leaving the Norfolk harbor he remarked that if the

submarine had been lost in the area the MIZAR was being assigned to,

that there was almost no hope of recovering her intact. But he also

pointed out that the techniques and equipment on board had advanced

since the THRESHER search and would get a real test in the coming search.

A following sea pushed the MIZAR out into the Atlantic for the first

four days, keeping the decks clear of traffic except for the two

intrepid scientists who had to climb out on top of the wellhouse and hook

up one of the antennas. But inside the ship was a flurry of activity as

scientists and crewmen searched for gear and equipment hurriedly brought

aboard in Norfolk. Many items like schematics, drawings, parts and

spare parts had been left behind in and on desks, file cabinets and even

at home in the rush.

Hour after hour "Buck" Buchanan and Bob Patterson attempted to put the

missing pieces together with the help of NRL's home office in Washington,

while other team members put together the many complex parts and circuits

of the "fish."

The "fish" is a 1400 poind metal cage approximately eight feet long

and three feet high with a magnatometer perched at the end of a two foot

tail. Mounted in the open "body" of the "fish" are two powerful strobe

(electronic flash) units, side-looking sonar, bottom-looking sonar,

battery cases, a motion picture camera and a TV camera. All of this

equipment is linked to a control cyclinder which relays commands from the

laboratory to the individual units and transmits data from the units to

the lab. This is done via the steel cable that not only lowers and

raises the fish from the ocean depths, but also acts as the "fish's"

-more-

umbilical cord. In the MIZAR's number one hold are two spare reels of cable, each reel over four miles long!

The cyclinders that house these sophisticated pieces of electronics gear are thick-walled, specially constructed steel cyclinders, designed to stand the pressures over three miles down!

On the way out to the search area, the equipment, from its circuit-board compenents, tiny transistors, capacitors and resistors, to the oscilliscopes, meters, and computers are check and rechecked, aligned, balanced and tested separately and as they are placed in the overall system.

Belying the apparent confusion in the lab spaces is a "Plan Of the Day" (POD) issued by Dr. Buchanan which sets forth the many jobs to be done that day in order of importance. This is one of the many places where the team concept manifests itself.

When John P. (Jack) Campbell, an Oceanographic Technician, see a note calling for a test run on the ship's sonar, he simply starts running the test and tells the GOLD team captain, Bob Patterson, the results. This is duely noted for Dr. Buchanan to see when his BLUE team takes over. A POD note to recharge the battery cells is noted by H. Bernard (Bernie) Lindstrom, a Mechanical Engineer, and any team member knows what Bernie is doing by simply looking at the POD. But each team member does more than his share as Electronics Technician Charles Griggs helps Motion Picture Technician Gless Worthington load his underwater camera and Research Geodesist Leslie L. Cunningham and Explosives Supervisor Jason H. Taylor cut out a bais-relief map of the bottom area they are searching. Electronics Engineer Lloyd S. Greenfield programs the sonar computer and

-more-

7

then helps Electronics Engineer Frank E. Acker check a component in the
control cyclinder. MIZAR Chief Electrician Joseph L. Davi helps Bernie
Lindstrom check out a power line while another scientist tries to find
batteries to power a crewmember's short wave radio.

As the weather clears the crew moves on deck to check out the cable
winch and ready it for the operation, check out the hydrallic doors in
the wellhouse and the pullies which guide the cable. The "fish" is
readied for its first dip in the water--this one with the bottles empty--
as last minute course corrections come to the bridge from the Navigational
Aids Room, bringing the ship to the search starting point. With the
ship barely moving, the "fish" is lowered down the hole into the water
until it approaches the bottom, over 1500 fathoms down! The "fish" is
then brought up and the water-tight integrity of the bottles is checked.
Then there are a series of brief "swims" with the "fish" as each
individual cyclinder is loaded with its assigned instrument and checked out.

After each "swim" minor adjustments and repairs are made and the final
problems are eliminated. During one of these "swims", there was a graphic
example of how great the water pressure is and what it can do. One of the
bottles, fortunately empty, developed a leak and before the caps came off,
equaliziang the pressure, the almost one inch thick cyclinder had caved
in at the middle like an empty soda can that has had its sides crushed in.

As we approach the operating area everyone is on the lookout for debris
and several false alarms are caused by floats from fishing nets that have
floated many thousands of miles on the ocean's currents.

-more-

7

As we reached the search starting point a strange sight appears on the horizon--a ship. It is the first ship that has been seen since leaving the Norfolk area although several Navy P3V's have been spotted flying overhead. The ship is identified as the Navy's oceanographic survey ship COMPASS ISLAND which dwarfs the MIZAR. The COMPASS ISLAND is finishing a map of the ocean bottom to help guide us in our search and some added help in the person of five Westinghouse scientists and their equipment. The MIZAR's Chief Steward, Charlie Wright Jr., does a little fast shuffling and the berthing and feeding of the new men is arranged. Ship's Purser Ernest E. Becker, who had veen taking the weekend sun, makes the appropriate entries on the sailing list as First Ofricer Mangual and Boatswain Herbert Hill make sure their equipment is brought aboard and properly stowed.

Captain Hobbs and Dr. Buchanan coordinate the lowering of the fish into the water while Second Officer and Navigator Lawrence F. Flynn takes the ship down the path charted by Les Cunningham.

Even the navigating of the ship is a team effort. In addition to compass and sun readings taken by the ship's officers, the Navigatinal Aids team from NavoceanO gives ship's position readings by using the Navigational Satellites and the newly instituted OMEGA system. As the NavSats pass a certain known point, they transmit data which is fed into a computer along with the ship's speed and bearing, current and wind data and time.

-more-

This data is converted by the computer into degrees, minutes and seconds of longitude and latitude. OMEGA uses four stations to give ships continuous readings accurate to within yards in any kind of weather.

As sonar makes a bar graph of the ocean bottom the fish is travelling over and the side-looking sonar feeds its contacts through a computer, the motion picture camera is taking a series of photographs at timed intervals controlled in the lab. The 114° angle of the camera's lens enables it to photograph a wide area of the bottom relatively free from distortion. Light for the camera is provided by two electronic flash units located on the front and back of the fish and controlled by the same impulse that controls the camera trigger. These quartz bulbs are capable of standing the great ocean pressures while giving off a brilliant, clear light so necessary in deep water. In scaning an area where the shallowist point is over 1500 fathoms, you must realize that there is almost no light whatsoever near the bottom and much of the bottom is shrouded in total darkness. Thus the strobes, powered by the fish's bottled batteries, provide the first light ever to shine on this mysterious ocean bottom.

The fish stays down until the batteries run down and/or the film runs out and except for the daily garbage run outside the search area, the ship continues to move slowly along its assigned path.

As the fish is lowered and brought up, the cable is constantly being checked for breaks in the outer sheathing cable. All cable breaks are quickly wrapped with tape to prevent the strands from

-more-

unravelling and each taped section is watched carefully for signs of wear.

A small device suspended from the bottom of the fish tells at what angle the fish is moving in the water in relation to the ship's beam.

Ready to lower the fish into the hole, it is first raised up to the top of the wellhouse until it fits snugly against the bottom of its silvered cradel. Then the deck-level doors slide ponderously open, revealing foam-capped, translucent blue water rising and falling within the well. Even the red-leaded sides of the well glow as the crystal blue water covers the slowly decending fish and its cradle. As the duo reach the bottom of the well, the fish "swims" free of the cradle and begins its cable-tow descend toward the dark ocean depths. The hydralic doors slide shut leaving only the unreeling cable in view.

In the Lab, the pings of sonar mingle with the whir of computers, the clatter of typewriters, the clicking of counters, the flashing of light across oscilliscope faces and the winking of digital clocks. Eyes flash from the TV screen monitoring the cable, coming off the cable drum , to the counter indicating the amount of cable, out to the o'scope screen showing the relationship of the fish to the ocean bottom. On charts in the lab, Navigation Center and the bridge, colored, sharp pencils and compasses keep tabs on the slow moving ship and its fish-like apendage. In the engine room, men work dilligently to keep the twin screws turning at precisely the rpm's relayed through the bridge from the lab. Film glides slowly through the processing

-more-

tank while in another room team members peer carefully as already developed images roll ever-so-slowly past.

The Search is not a matter of hours, days or weeks. It bears little relation to time, rather it is a series of charts, graphs, photographs and taped impulses and the constant spinning of ship's propellers. The flickering of numbers on the digital clock only provide a reference number in coordinating the stream of data and the flourescent lights of the lab and sleeping quarters erode the concept of day and night. The sight of bare-chested Les Cunningham coming down from the main deck into the lab from his off-watch exercise makes one aware of the passing time.

Meals provide a welcome break as well as signaling the end of one shift. A well-balanced menu offering a variety of main courses with vegetables and potatoes or rice prepared to taste are a trademark of the MSTSLANT ships and despite the MIZAR's small size there is no cutback on the quality or quantity of well prepared meals. The same is true of the living and working spaces throughout the ship, freshly painted, clean and well lit. The crewmembers smile when this is remarked upon and remind you of the letter a young sailor sent to his mother after sending several weeks aboard his first ship. In this plaintive missive he reminded her of how he had chosen the Navy because its ships were always so clean and neat. "Now I know who keeps them this way," was his message.

Safety, especially shipboard safety, is something you are constantly aware of and there are written and physical reminders throughout the ship. The first thing that catches your eye on

-more-

7

the bridge is a large sign which states "SAFETY FIRST, SCHEDULE
SECOND--YOUR SCHEDULE IS FLEXIBLE, YOUR SHIP IS NOT." Crewmen
painting passageways or chipping paint on deck wear protective
goggles and all outlets and plugs are three-pronged (the third
prong is for grounding). Handrails, lifejackets and helmets
are in evidence throughout and drills are coordinated with the
scientists who, along with the crew, appreciate the seriousness
and necessity for the "just-in-case" breaks into their work.

A crew's lounge is slowly taking shape in the compartment
just forward of the galley, but the major work will have to wait
until the ship's next yard period. The MIZAR was concerned for
many years with keeping its crew warm as it travelled to the
polar regions but many of its past four years as an oceanographic
research ship have been spent in much warmer climes. The lab
and adjoining scientific spaces are already air-conditioned as
are the scientists' quarters and the crews' spaces will be
converted during her next yard period.

-USN-

Teamwork helps Mizar find sub

Highly touted NMU crew and crack scientists track down lost sub Scorpion

Every morning seven men meet in a downtown building in Washington where they spend the greater part of each day going over hundreds of photographs. These men belong to a team of Navy experts whose job it is to piece together—from studying the photographs—exactly what happened to the ill-fated nuclear-powered submarine Scorpion. The photos were taken on the floor of the Atlantic Ocean about 10,000 feet beneath the hull of the naval oceanographic research ship Mizar.

Of course, the pictures may never reveal how the $40 million Scorpion met its doom. But the fact that the Mizar was able to pinpoint the location of the wreckage is as much a tribute to the skill and patience of the crew as to the efficiency of the highly sophisticated electronic equipment carried by the ship. "It was like looking for a contact lens in a haystack," said Chester L. Buchanan, chief scientist on the Mizar.

"The fish." The Mizar had played a key role in locating the attack submarine Thresher which sank in 8,400 feet of water off New England in April, 1963 and had been instrumental in locating the hydrogen bomb lost off the coast of Spain in 1966. In all probability, the 3,500-ton Scorpion never would have been found with the equipment used to search for the Thresher. Now the Mizar is equipped with a $75,000 "fish" that can spot objects on the ocean floor. The fish, a nine-foot long metal rack laden with detection gear and dragged by a three-quarter-inch cable 25 feet above the ocean bottom, is launched and retrieved through a 10-by-22-foot well in the ship's bottom.

Uses sonar beams. Suspended from the tail of the fish is a magnetometer, an instrument that measures the intensity of a magnetic field and senses the presence of metal objects. Sonar beams sweep out from the sides of the fish to locate underwater objects. During the first 18 weeks the Mizar searched for the Scorpion, she located only a bottle, a can and a metal plate. No one knew whether the plate was a part of the Scorpion but it led the Mizar to try again in the same area.

The ship searched a regular pattern, zigzagging across the Scorpion's projected track at a speed of little more than a mile an hour. She sailed first 40 miles on one side of the track, made a sharp turn and went 40 miles on the other side. In 145 days of searching, Mizar's cameras took more than 200,000 pictures—12,000 in the immediate area of the Scorpion. On her last try in the month of October the instruments showed that she had made contact. Photos developed in the early morning hours of October 30 confirmed that the Mizar had indeed found the Scorpion within three to five miles of where the metal plate had been spotted.

Crew cited by skipper. Capt. James D. Hobbs, skipper of the Mizar, paid tribute to the "skill and patience of every man aboard this ship. When you think of the infinite care and attention that must go into an operation of this kind, you cannot find enough words to salute a crew that makes a success of the job," Hobbs said. For coming through in fine style in the Scorpion operation, the officers and crew of the Mizar were presented with the first "Hard Charger" Award by Vice Admiral L. P. Ramage, Commander, Military Sea Transportation Service. The citation commended the skipper and crew for their accomplishments in locating the Scorpion, Thresher and the H-bomb.

The Mizar is an unusual ship, having been built originally as an ice-breaking supply ship for Arctic and Antarctic waters. She underwent a conversion to her present "search and research" use because of the Thresher disaster. Her 35-man unlicensed crew has been 90 per cent NMU since 1963, the year after Executive Order 10988 was signed by the late President John F. Kennedy. The Mirfak, her sistership, is also manned by a crew made up largely of NMU members and still operates as a resupply ship for MSTS vessels operating in the Arctic and Antarctic.

Great team. The scientists and seamen make a great team working together to accomplish their mission. The ship's crew has to navigate the vessel along precise headings so that the scientific crew headed up by chief scientist Buchanan can feed data into the computer aboard which will tell them exactly the area covered in the search. "I don't want to sound like a mutual admiration society," said Captain Hobbs, "but I have never sailed with a finer bunch of men."

The skipper, whose home is Baltimore, has a background of 20 years at sea, coming up the hawsepipe entirely in the service of the Military Sea Transportation Service. He is considered one of the most knowledgeable ships' officers in the field of Arctic seaborne operations. Bosun Herbert Hill, who has been aboard the ship for several years, regards the skipper as the kind of commanding officer the men "really put out for, because he knows what being a seamen is like."

If the mystery of the submarine Scorpion is ever unravelled, it will mainly be due to the fine cooperation and excellent seamanship found on board the Mizar during the time it took to track down the whereabouts of the lost sub.